Anti-Americanism
in Europe

Anti-Americanism in Europe
A Cultural Problem

Russell A. Berman

HOOVER INSTITUTION PRESS
Stanford University   Stanford, California

www.hoover.org

Hoover Institution Press Publication No. 527

First printing 2004
10   09   08   07   06   05   04   9   8   7   6   5   4   3   2   1

Manufactured in the United States of America
The paper used in this publication meets the minimum requirements
of American National Standard for Information Sciences—Permanence
of Paper for Printed Library Materials, ANSI Z39.48-1992. ∞

An earlier version of chapter 3, "Democratic War, Repressive Peace: On Really
Existing Anti-Americanism," appeared in German in the journal *Merkur*
("Demokratischer Krieg, repressiver Frieden: über den realexistierenden
Antiamerikanismus," *Merkur* 57 [July 2003]: 570–582); an earlier version of
chapter 4, "Saddam as Hitler," appeared in the journal *Telos* ("Saddam and Hitler:
Rethinking Totalitarianism," *Telos* 125 [Fall 2002]: 121–139).

Library of Congress Cataloging-in-Publication Data
Berman, Russell A., 1950–
    Anti-Americanism in Europe : a cultural problem / by Russell A. Berman.
        p.   cm. (Hoover Institution Press publication ; no. 527)
    Includes bibliographical references and index.
    ISBN 0-8179-4512-1 (alk. paper)
    1. Anti-Americanism—Europe.   2. Anti-Americanism—Germany.
3. Europe—Relations—United States.   4. United States—Relations—
Europe.   5. United States—Politics and government—2001—Public opinion.
I. Title.   II. Hoover Institution Press publication ; 527.
D1065.U5B44   2004
303.48′214073—dc22   2004001692

For Paul

Contents ✥

Acknowledgments ✖

This volume brings together five essays concerned with the aspects of European-American relations as they were redefined in the context of the Iraq war of 2003. I am grateful for the generous support of the Hoover Institution in the completion of this project.

Two of the chapters have appeared in other contexts. Chapter 3 was published in German in *Merkur*, and an earlier version of chapter 4 has appeared in *Telos*. The other chapters were written originally for conferences and anthologies. They have all been revised and present—such is my hope—a unified argument regarding a major issue of our time.

Introduction ❖

As the diplomatic relations between the United States and some of its traditional European allies grew strained after September 11, so too did the attitudes of Europeans regarding the United States decline considerably. Positive opinions of the United States dropped in France from 62 percent in 1999/ 2000 to 43 percent in June 2003, as reported by the Pew Global Attitudes Project (discussed in chapter 1). In Germany the fall was even more dramatic, from 78 percent to 45 percent, and in Spain, from 50 percent to 38 percent. One can clearly conclude that large majorities in key Western European countries have ceased to be positively predisposed to the United States.

Several objective and strategic factors help explain this growth in anti-Americanism. The collapse of the Soviet Union and the end of the cold war have meant that Western Europe no longer needs the protection of U.S. troops, which in turn makes a public anti-American rhetoric more permissible than in the past. In addition, as the United States emerged as the single superpower (a tendency long before 1989 but only explicit after the demise of the Soviet empire), it became a more obvious target; Europeans could resent American power more while also paradoxically expecting the United States to shoulder more international responsibilities.

In retrospect, the period between the fall of the Berlin wall on November 9, 1989, and the terrorist attacks in Washington, D.C., and New York City on September 11, 2001, can be viewed as a transition period in the emergence of a new international system, including a profound transformation of European attitudes toward the United States. The United States responded to terrorism robustly with the wars against the Taliban and against Saddam Hussein. Although a minority of Europeans genuinely supported these wars, there was also extensive opposition, based on an underlying inclination toward a policy of appeasement. This difference heightened tensions across the Atlantic. For the United States, September 11 indicated the need for strategies to reduce security threats. For many Europeans, September 11 was taken as evidence of how American behavior elicits hostility and how it would therefore be up to Americans to repent and change their ways. September 11 and its aftermath proved to be a turning point in European anti-Americanism, which has become an increasingly open and acceptable attitude.

Yet this transformation of European attitudes regarding the United States would not have been as pointed had it not been for another factor, related to the strategic post–cold war changes. As the process of European unification progressed, anti-Americanism proved to be a useful ideology for the definition of a new European identity. Currently, the main way Europe defines itself as European is precisely by underscoring its difference from the United States. To be sure, this is not the only way to define Europe, nor must it remain that way in the future. If the European political class were to speak out more forcefully against anti-Americanism, other understandings of "Europe" might be possible. Yet in the meantime, treating the

United States as the alternative to Europe—rather than as a part-ner—retains considerable attraction.

Writing in February 2002, after the success of the Afghani-stan war, the author Salman Rushdie commented: "Anybody who has visited Britain and Europe, or followed the public con-versation there during the past five months, will have been struck, even shocked, by the depth of anti-American feeling among large segments of the population, as well as the news media. Western anti-Americanism is an altogether more petulant phenomenon than its Islamic counterpart and, oddly, far more personalized. Muslim countries don't like America's power, its 'arrogance,' its success; in the non-American West, the main objection seems to be to American *people*."[1] Anti-Americanism, in other words, may take this or that policy dispute as a pretext for criticism about the United States. European anti-American-ism, however, involves a hostility that goes far beyond specific policies and entails a much larger and generalized disdain for America and Americans. It has elements of ideology and obses-sion; it is cultural and irrational; and it is likely to remain a fea-ture of relations between the United States and Europe for the foreseeable future. Particularly in the cultural elite, but by no means only there, the animosity toward the United States is deep. As celebrated German theater director Peter Zadek has put it with admirable clarity: "I think that it is cowardly that many people distinguish between the American people and the current American administration. The Bush administration was more or less democratically elected, and it had the support of the majority of Americans in its Iraq war. One can therefore be

1. Salman Rushdie, "February 2002: Anti-Americanism," in Rushdie, *Step across This Line: Collected Nonfiction 1992–2002* (New York: Random House, 2002), 343.

against the Americans, just as most of the world was against the Germans in the Second World War. In this sense, I am an anti-American."[2] This one example stands for many instances of the European culture of anti-Americanism.

This book explores various dimensions of contemporary European anti-Americanism. Because anti-Americanism is a cultural problem—albeit with enormous consequences for policy—the tools of cultural analysis are necessary to understand it. Chapter 1 examines several recent surveys in order to determine the quantitative scope of anti-American sentiment, especially since September 11. The focus is on Germany, the key continental European ally during the cold war but also the site of the initial dispute over Iraq policy. German attitudes to the United States are interesting in various ways: the positive image of the United States has declined there more rapidly than in other European countries, whereas on various cultural questions, the Germans (or the West Germans, at least) are more like Americans than other Europeans. German anti-Americanism has features that are peculiarly German, as well as epitomizing a larger European phenomenon.

Because anti-Americanism is so much a matter of culture, the subsequent chapters examine various cultural traditions, intellectual historical lineages, and the attitudes of members of the cultural elite. Chapter 2 describes how anti-Americanism goes beyond rational debates over policy—a critic of this or that American policy is hardly necessarily an anti-American—and takes on an obsessive character. Anti-Americanism operates like a prejudice and a stereotype in the sense that it is impervious to rational arguments or factual proof. In general, European anti-

2. "Kulturkampf? Ich bin dabei: Spiegelgespräch," *Der Spiegel*, July 14, 2003.

Americanism has deep cultural roots, stretching back for centuries. The discovery of a "new world" challenged the European worldview and self-understanding, leading to various preconceptions about America: too violent, too democratic, too powerful. In addition, this chapter suggests a typology of three different variants of anti-Americanism: a predemocratic cultural elitism that dismisses American mass culture; the antidemocratic legacy of the Communist attacks on the United States, left over from the cold war; and a postdemocratic resentment that the United States retains an independence and sovereignty while the European nations submit increasingly to transnational forms of governance.

Chapter 3 examines the shape of anti-Americanism in the debates over the Iraq war. The sudden rage that erupted against the United States in major Western European cities, examined closely, is symptomatic of the emerging European identity. Although critics of the war regularly warned against upheavals around the world, it was primarily in Western Europe that anti-American demonstrators took to the streets. By supporting a policy of appeasement toward Saddam Hussein and opposing the democratization of Iraq, the Europeans, in the streets and in some governments, shed light on the political substance at stake. Their reluctance to criticize authoritarian regimes has led them to a position hostile to any "regime change." Indeed, for European anti-Americanism, no regime is so bad that it could ever warrant supporting the United States in bringing that regime to an end: not in Serbia, not in Afghanistan, and not in Iraq.

Chapter 4 explores the roots of anti-Americanism in this reluctance to criticize bad regimes for fear of siding with the United States. The historical and metaphorical frame around the two Iraq wars—the comparison of Saddam and Hitler—turns out to be quite illuminating on this point. When all is said and done, the world did not rush to oppose either dictator; on the contrary, appeasement and a certain reality denial defined the relationship to Nazi Germany as much as it did to Saddam's Iraq. For Western Europeans, and perhaps for many others, it has always been more comfortable to ignore the violence of totalitarian states. Because the United States sets a higher moral standard in a way that causes discomfort to the appeasers, it becomes the target of resentment: another source of anti-Americanism.

The fifth and final chapter looks at another variation of anti-Americanism: the movement against globalization. Antiglobalization has become the most prominent form of anticapitalism since the collapse of Communism. As post-Communist anticapitalism, it overlaps considerably with anti-Americanism. This chapter examines the rhetoric of anti-Americanism in the writings of the French philosopher and social theorist Jean Baudrillard and the Indian author Arundhati Roy; Roy's anti-American writings have been widely circulated in Western Europe in the context of the wars in Afghanistan and Iraq. Both writers lodge the critique of the United States within frameworks of antiglobalization. Their positions are contrasted with an alternative judgment from an earlier historical period, that of the German philosopher Theodor Adorno, some of whose writings on the legacy of Nazi Germany explore the overlap between anti-Americanism and antimodernization. Adorno suggests that the greater orientation toward democratic and free market structures in England and America explains their historical willingness to confront totalitarianism, just as continental European statism contributed to a predisposition to collaboration. This thesis implies that contemporary Western European anti-Americanism is not just a response to U.S. policies in Afghanistan and

Iraq but a much deeper rejection of those free market principles that Germans sometimes call "American conditions."

Anti-Americanism is not going to disappear in Western Europe overnight. The debate that erupted in the wake of September 11 has not been just a friendly disagreement. A deep divide has emerged. This book is intended as a contribution to understanding this important ideological challenge.

San Francisco, August 2003

1 ✿

The German Perception of the United States since September 11 and the European Context

When George W. Bush visited Berlin in May 2002, he attracted large and hostile demonstrations. The recent war in Afghanistan had been very unpopular in Germany and elsewhere in Western Europe, amplifying a diffuse anti-Americanism associated with various policy decisions: the U.S. rejection of the Kyoto Treaty, the opposition to the International Criminal Court, and other aspects of U.S. foreign policy, especially support for Israel. Yet when Bush visited several formerly Communist countries in Central and Eastern Europe during the subsequent fall, his visit elicited friendly, pro-American crowds, especially in Vilnius and Bucharest.

It would be difficult to argue that American policies had changed in the interim between the two visits in a way that could explain a shift in the foreign perception of the United States. On the contrary, what is clearly at stake is the phenomenon of how the United States is viewed differently in different countries. In other words, the perception of the United States is not, or not only, a function of the external factor of the character of American policy. Rather, the perception of the United States in a particular country is very much framed by internal factors, sets of local circumstances, cultural legacies, and political habits.

It is therefore plausible to surmise that the warm reception accorded Bush in the formerly Communist capitals reflected the local memories of the indispensable leadership role the United States had played in opposing Russian domination during the cold war, leading up to the turning point of 1989. In this chapter, however, the other side of the comparison is at stake: the internal factors that determine the German perception of the United States, especially the attitudes toward America since September 11. How have factors specific to German culture and history influenced the perception of the United States? And how does the German view of the United States fit into the larger European context?

The Question of Perceptions

Before proceeding to German public opinion data, however, it is important to consider why Americans have become so pointedly concerned with foreign perceptions of the United States. Various developments have contributed to a heightened attention among Americans to their image abroad. The collapse of the Soviet Union and the emergence of the United States as the sole superpower—a tendency under way long before 1989 but only fully apparent afterward—imply a changed position of the United States in the world and hence an interest in understanding the image of the United States abroad. If it is the case that the single superpower cannot, ultimately, avoid global responsibilities—otherwise it ceases to be a superpower, after all—then it is in the rational interest of the superpower to understand how it is viewed around the world.

In addition to this pragmatic approach to the question of perception, one can identify a cultural-critical approach as well: contemporary culture is often defined by a so-called mass culture that tends to place greater weight on questions of image, and therefore perception, than on matters of substance. It follows that increasing concern is directed to the response to policy, how it appears, or what "spin" it is given, rather than what the policy achieves directly. This cultural problem is related to the extensive impact of the media and the culture industry.

A third context surrounding the interest in the perception of the United States, of course, is a direct effect of September 11. The attacks on the World Trade Center and the Pentagon are widely understood as attacks on the United States as a whole (i.e., on the American way of life) symbolized by the two buildings. The growing curiosity about the perception of the United States overseas represents an effort to explore the roots of this animosity as a way to explain the terrorist attacks. Without discounting possible benefits of this approach, it should be noted, of course, that this line of thinking does tend to impute a legitimizing motivation to the September 11 attackers. Rather than seeing the terrorists as isolated extremists, driven by idiosyncratic fanaticism, this approach implicitly links them to much larger cultural perceptions. The policy consequence of this assumption is that, in order to prevent further terrorist attacks, the United States should change its image abroad by changing its ways—its policies and its "way of life"—rather than by pursuing the suppression and eradication of specific terrorist networks.

This policy implication indicates how deeply politicized the debate over perception has become. It is useful to recall that there have been other periods during which the United States faced considerable opposition or anti-Americanism overseas, most notably in the context of the cold war in the 1950s and early 1960s. Yet despite the cliché of the ugly American, the foreign perception of the United States did not expand into a major concern in domestic debates, for several reasons. At that time, the United States was not the single superpower but faced, on the contrary, the Soviet Union with its very real aspirations for global power. This in turn implied that expressions of anti-Americanism could be attributed, properly or not, to a real-world power conflict rather than to an elusive matter of image management. Moreover, the American culture of the 1950s and 1960s was certainly less image-obsessed than we are a half century later. In addition, the United States had not suffered any blow to its sense of security on the level of the September 11 attacks. Perhaps a comparison might be drawn to the Soviet acquisition of the nuclear bomb; suddenly the American sense of security associated with being the sole nuclear power disappeared. In that cultural context, however, the political response was to ask about real espionage: how they spy on us. In today's image-obsessed culture, by way of contrast, we are concerned with appearance: how they view us, and why they do not like us.

One further context explains the current interest in foreign perceptions of the United States. Until the debates over the Vietnam War, an extensive bipartisan foreign policy consensus prevailed. Anti-Americanism overseas could not be transformed into political capital for domestic use. In contrast, today that foreign policy consensus has broken down, in part due to the end of the cold war, the single superpower status, and the lack of clear unanimity regarding an appropriate strategy, evidenced in the debates over unilateralism and multilateralism. United States politics in general have become more divisive, ideological, and acrimonious. To some extent this changing character of domestic political style can be explained by party realignments, to some extent by deeper cultural changes. In any case, in the context of a missing foreign policy consensus and an increas-

ingly agonistic public debate, anti-Americanism abroad, interpreted as opposition to specific American policies, gains much
greater resonance within American politics as part of the domestic partisan competition, in a way, for example, that anti-American demonstrators in Europe or Latin America in the 1950s
could never achieve.

Because anti-Americanism in the past could be attributed to
Communist activism, it had little partisan value in the centrist
American political scene. With the collapse of the Soviet Union,
however, anti-Americanism could paradoxically take on an
appearance of legitimacy, to the extent that it could no longer
be dismissed as a Communist artifice and, on the contrary, could
now be accepted as a reasonable response to particular United
States policies, especially when those policies are themselves
already contested in the increasingly partisan domestic debates.
Therefore the putative reasonableness and policy specificity of
anti-Americanism become key assumptions for domestic political debate. These assumptions are, however, simultaneously subject to critical skepticism, in the sense that expressions of
sentiments hostile to the United States can be questioned: are
they really driven by U.S. policy or are there other motivations?
This is precisely why questions regarding the origins of anti-
Americanism are raised: do negative images of the United States
in general, or anti-American demonstrations in particular, represent reasoned objections to U.S. government actions (in the
sense that changing a policy would establish goodwill), or are
they primarily expressions of local circumstances (which are
likely to generate hostility regardless of U.S. policy shifts)?
Should hostile expressions in Germany be treated as cogent
objections to misguided policies emanating from Washington,
or are they symptomatic of aspects of German national history
and, therefore, not directly pertinent to formulation of policy in

the United States (except perhaps to the extent that such policy refers specifically to Germany)? To sort out answers to these questions, it becomes necessary to inquire into the specific local circumstances in which particular images of the United States develop. The contrast between the hostile demonstrations in Berlin and the friendly demonstrations in Vilnius and Bucharest is a case in point. In such cases, the image of the United States obviously involves the acting out of local issues, rather than a considered deliberation of particular policies.

Cultural Contexts

Germany is a rich and complex case with regard to the formulation of perspectives on the United States. Few countries have had such intense and extended interactions as have Germany and the United States. Germany and the United States were opponents in the two world wars, and whereas West Germany drew close to the United States, East Germany was a key member of the Soviet bloc, with its own set of anti-American attitudes. In other words, the twentieth-century legacy of German-American history involves considerable grounds for negative predispositions. Although elsewhere in the formerly Communist states of Eastern Europe, the anti-Communist foreign policy of the cold war United States translates into pro-American sympathies today, a comparable post-Communist bonus does not appear to apply in the new states of unified Germany (i.e., the territories that formerly composed the German Democratic Republic). Although the former East Germans are surely better off than the populations of any of the other new democracies, they do not participate in the same positive estimation of the United States. On the contrary, there is a specifically German continuity from pre-1989 Communist anti-

East German dont share the pos. views US
other E. Eur. do.

Americanism to post-Communist anti-Americanism, which has been particularly relevant, given the role of the former Communist Party—the Party of Democratic Socialism (PDS)—and its ability to influence the larger German political landscape.

The twentieth-century legacy of German-American relations therefore includes grounds for suspicion but also a strong history of affection and idealization. The post–Second World War experience of Americans by West Germans was crucial and transformative. Although Americans were not genuinely welcomed as liberators in 1945, the protection afforded by the United States against an expansionist Soviet empire generated much affection among West Germans. From the Berlin airlift of 1948 through the enormously resonant speech by President Kennedy in West Berlin, with his assertion "Ich bin ein Berliner," to President Reagan's call to "tear down" the Berlin wall, the relationship between the United States and the Federal Republic of Germany grew strong and stable and with it so did connections between American and West German society. American popular culture and American scholarship both had profound influence on postwar German culture. Indeed, even the West German student movement of the 1960s, which articulated deep criticisms of aspects of American foreign policy, was itself formatively influenced by the character of the youth culture and the student movement that had developed in the United States.

Thus German perspectives on the United States developed against a background of a mixture of negative and positive attitudes. Although these biases derive from the twentieth-century historical experience of encounters with the United States, they also build on much deeper cultural-historical stances: the eighteenth-century German enlightenment idealization of the experiment of the American republic and the nineteenth-century

German romantic suspicion of capitalism and democracy.[1] Yet, for the matter at hand—German perceptions of the United States after September 11—the specific history of German attitudes to the United States is arguably less important than German views of their own past. Contemporary, unified Germany maintains a largely critical attitude to the militarism of its own national history and tends to draw de facto pacifist lessons: war is regarded as the absolute evil, military solutions to international problems are shunned at all costs, and therefore any current war—such as the United States' war in Afghanistan or Iraq—is typically viewed through the lens of the German experience in the world wars. This leads to the projection of German metaphors onto American policy: in the extreme, George W. Bush is equated with Adolf Hitler (as in the grotesque remark of the former German minister of justice Herta Däubler-Gmelin). Variants of this equation are common (e.g., the suggestion that the attacks of September 11 were planned or facilitated by the Americans and were intended to play the same role that the burning of the Reichstag did for the consolidation of Nazi power). In these cases, the genuine psychic burden of the guilty German past is presumably temporarily lifted through the accusation that the Americans of today are, ultimately, no better than the Germans of the Nazi era. This is as much a case of judging the present through the lens of the national past as is—with alternative results—the East European, pro-American willingness to see current U.S. policy in light of the U.S. foreign policy of the cold war era. The German projection of its national history onto current events can even be taken one step further: not only by identifying today's Americans with Hitler-era Germans

---

1. Cf. Dan Diner, *America in the Eyes of the Germans: An Essay on Anti-Americanism*, trans. Allison Brown (Princeton: Markus Wiener, 1996).

but also by drawing a connection between the Anglo-American air war in the Second World War and the bombing of Afghanistan and Iraq. Needless to say, the equation entails a massive minimization of what took place during the Second World War, and it ignores the precise targeting capabilities of new missile technologies. The key point, however, is the remarkable degree to which Germans see current events as repetitions of their own national past, even identifying with the victim status of the targets of American foreign policy.

There is one further dimension of the German situation that intrudes on current perceptions of the United States: the process of European unification. An aspiration to develop a unified continental political system has deep historical roots. In its current form, it commenced after the Second World War as a project for a common economic market in Western Europe. European institutions have gradually grown more political (i.e., not solely economic) and more regulatory. Some political powers of national governments have been transferred to European institutions, including the maintenance of a currency: the euro is now the coin of the realm through much of Europe, and monetary policy has thereby ceased to be a national prerogative. In addition, Europe has expanded its membership, largely due to the fall of the iron curtain and the opportunity to integrate Central and Eastern European states. Although the United States generally has supported the process of European unification, a subtle shift has taken place, particularly since 1989. Although European unification once represented part of the bulwark that the West presented against Soviet expansionism, after the collapse of Russian hegemony the European Union began to define itself in relation to the United States (i.e., as an alternative to the United States in a hypothetically multipolar world). Anti-American sentiment has become the vehicle for the expression of this new European identity.

Meanwhile, the European Union suffers from a so-called democracy deficit: political powers have been shifted to a bureaucracy largely shielded from public scrutiny and electoral control. This bureaucratization of Europe means that the process of unification has little capacity to appeal to the ideals or loyalty of a pan-European citizenry; so far, individuals in much of Europe typically remain loyal to their respective nation-states rather than to the abstract superstate. Germans, however, given their troubled national past, have been among the strongest supporters of the European unification process: becoming more European is a way to become less German. The central lesson on which this unification process has been based involves the presumed urgency to overcome the egoism of individual nations and replace it with multilateral cooperation. This multilateralism entails a renunciation of elements of national sovereignty in the name of greater cooperation among nation-states. Although many continental European states are prepared to take this step, some are reluctant to do so (especially the United Kingdom), and, in any case, the United States has shown little interest in subjecting itself to international governance structures: hence the debate over multilateralism and unilateralism that erupted in the context of the Iraq war. This material frequently colors German views of the United States. The United States and West Germany maintained a deep alliance through the cold war decades, and unified Germany has inherited its role in this partnership. However, unified Germany has also inherited another aspect of the older West German political culture: a willingness to subordinate its specific national interests to larger international, especially European, processes. Because of its role in the two world wars, Germany today is predisposed to renounce elements of its national sovereignty in order to become a good European. Public opinion in Germany is therefore particularly suspicious of the American reluctance to cede power to international governance structures. In this case, it is not, strictly speaking, an internal German factor that shapes the perception of the United States, but a regional process: the relationship of Europe, of which Germany is a key component, to the United States.

Representation of the United States in German Print Media

Several surveys of representations of the United States and of public opinion regarding foreign policy can help shed light on these matters. The study *America's Image Abroad*, conducted at Michigan State University, provides data concerning the representation of the September 11 attacks and related issues during the autumn of 2001.[2] To be sure, one should be cautious not to overstate the significance of these data. Although the study surveys several key organs of the German print media, both daily newspapers and weekly news magazines, it does not include electronic media, through which large sectors of the public receive their news information. Moreover, the data are not corrected for circulation size. References to the United States in newspapers with only local or regional readership (e.g., *Augsburger Allgemeine, Südwest Presse*) are put on the same level as references in the large-circulation de facto national newspapers (e.g., *Frankfurter Allgemeine, Süddeutsche Zeitung*) and in the influential weekly publications *(Der Spiegel, Die Zeit)*. In order to extrapolate from representations in the various press organs to

2. Vladimir Shlapentokh and Joshua Woods, *America's Image Abroad* (forthcoming).

public opinion in general, one would have to factor in these various circulation profiles and their implications for readership influence. Germany has a variegated media environment, and it is not uncommon for readers, at least those in the educated strata, to draw on combinations of these publications. At the other end of the literacy spectrum, however, significant strata of the public only read the mass-distribution boulevard press, such as *Die Bildzeitung.*

Although the data collected cannot be directly mapped onto public opinion, they do at least present an initial rough cut of the representation of the United States under the impact of September 11 and as such provide some important insights into German political culture. Particularly dramatic are the data collected regarding the question, "How should America respond to the September 11 events?" The aggregate findings display a profile polarized around diametrically opposed positions, with 23 percent of the press comments attributed to the negative "Do not use military tactics or force. Do not declare a war against terrorism or those deemed responsible for it," whereas 37.3 percent are counted for "Use military force or bombings against the governments, states, or groups that harbor or support those responsible for September 11. Make no compromises with these governments." The policy at stake, obviously, involved the pursuit of a war against terrorism in the form of the campaign against the Taliban regime of Afghanistan. German press representations appear, on first glance, to tilt toward the promilitary and, in this historical context, pro-American option.

The ratio of 37:23, however, is to some extent an arbitrary result of the structure of the content analysis. If one takes into account the numerous other responses, none of which on its own gets above 8 percent, and allocates them reasonably between the two camps, the overall polarization becomes starker. Thus one can attribute proposals to alleviate poverty, change foreign policy, "pause and reflect soberly," and work with the United Nations, to the antimilitary camp. Alternatively, calls to improve intelligence, gather credible evidence, work with the entire world, and attack (only) terrorist camps might be counted on the military side of the ledger (arguably, some of these items belong to the antimilitary camp, but that attribution would only amplify the results of this exercise). Making these assumptions, one finds a split of 45.3 percent against the use of force and 48.8 percent supporting it.

This structural polarization is corroborated by an accompanying tendency. The data display an increased polarization in October 2001, as measured against September 2001. In other words, after the initial shock of September 11, and as public debate unfolded, positions tended to harden into two opposing camps. Thus (looking now only at the major categories and bracketing the smaller, peripheral ones), expressions of opposition to American use of military force rose from 18.6 percent of press comments in September 2001 to 30.1 percent in October 2001 while support for military force grew from 26.3 percent to 46.9 percent. In fact, support grew to 75 percent in December 2001, although this number is based on a much smaller evidence pool, and in any case, the Afghanistan campaign had largely ended at this point. (It therefore made little sense to oppose the use of force any longer, so that a reasonable comparison with the data from previous months becomes difficult.)

These data suggest a complex representational process in the German print media. In the aftermath of September 11, it is clear that there was much support for American use of force as a proper response, and not limited specifically to terrorist camps. Nonetheless, there is also evidence of dispute and polarization. The treatment of the issue in the press was split nearly equally.

Even in the context of the war against the Taliban—where the case for a connection to September 11 was always much stronger and clearer than it was later with the highly contested war policy in Iraq—nearly half the press treatment opposed the unlimited military solution. To be sure, there was evidence of a concurrent pro-American predisposition, and the antiwar opposition represented a (slight) minority of items in the content analyses. Still this minority indicated a nontrivial antiwar potential: precisely the potential that turned into the crowds at the anti-Bush demonstrations in the subsequent May and on which German Chancellor Gerhard Schroeder made his electoral calculation a year later, when he chose to oppose the intervention in Iraq.

The findings for other aspects of the content analysis add interesting detail to this hypothesis of a German press prepared to tilt toward the United States in a post–September 11 solidarity effect but already displaying signs of reluctance or even resistance. Thus with regard to the question of how Germany should respond to September 11, a clear majority of 51.4 percent of the press comments indicate support for working with the United States, even in military responses. There is, curiously perhaps, more support for Germany to cooperate with the United States, even in military steps, than there is for the United States to pursue such military steps. One can surmise that for the German public sphere, the need for identification with the United States was even stronger than a judgment on the particular political means (i.e., some of the reluctance to support military initiatives could be set aside in order to maintain loyalty to the United States). This too points to a post–September 11 solidarity effect. If one also counts calls for cooperation with the United States in restricted military responses (terrorist camps only) or nonmilitary responses, then the hypothetically pro-American evidence

count comes to 83.9 percent. However, it is perhaps more reasonable to assume that these variants—restricted military and
nonmilitary responses—in the context of the German debate on
the Afghanistan war in effect represented positions defined as
opposed to U.S. government policy. If one combines these data
(9.9 percent and 7.7 percent) with a marginal call for an independent German strategy (0.6 percent) and other opposition to
support for the United States in general (1.1 percent), one dis-
covers a rejectionist field of a not insignificant 19.3 percent.
This, it would seem, suggests that the notion of universal solidarity with the United States in the immediate aftermath of September 11 is not tenable. From the very start, there was a vocal
minority position in precise and explicit opposition to the policy
pursued by the American government (i.e., the attack on the
Taliban regime in Afghanistan). It is fair to speculate that if
nearly one-fifth of the German press representation of the issue
in the context of the Afghanistan War (where the case was both
clearest and temporally closest to the September 11 attacks)
implied an adversarial attitude toward the United States, then it
was plausible to predict that a much greater hesitation would
emerge regarding American-led military solutions in the less
obvious case of Iraq.

Other aspects of German public culture are apparent in the
data. The significance of moderate centrist views is evident in
the fact that 87.4 percent of the press reports designate Osama
bin Laden or Islamic fundamentalists as the perpetrators of September 11. This is proof of the reasonable and democratic predisposition of German public life. Nonetheless, the fringe
position that attributes the September 11 attacks to Israeli special forces is represented minimally but noticeably, and equally
on the Left (*Die Tageszeitung*) and the Right (*Die Bildzeitung*). The
convergence of left anti-Zionism and traditional right antisemi-

tism is certainly not a solely German phenomenon, but it takes place closer to the center of public debate in Germany than it does elsewhere. Although these two newspapers can be taken to represent the respective ends of the political spectrum under discussion, they are surely not in any sense part of extremist subcultures.

The data on understandings of the root causes of September 11 attribute 12.4 percent to religious fanaticism and 18.0 percent to Islamic fundamentalism, making a total of 30.4 percent. Moreover this attribution increases from September 2001 to October 2001, presumably an effect of the case against the Taliban being made with increasing cogency. Nonetheless, in September 2001 nearly 30 percent of the references to the September 11 attacks blamed them on U.S. policies, be it a matter of the support for Israel or the earlier support for the Mujahideen against the Soviets in Afghanistan. In other words, the significant support for the United States in the German public sphere was again accompanied by varying degrees of reluctance, rejection, or opposition even immediately after September 11. Despite the 58.0 percent describing September 11 as "an attack against freedom, democracy, humanity, or the civilized world," there is remarkable balance between the assertions of a conflict of civilizations (10.2 percent) and denials of this conflict (11.4 percent). That is to say, underneath a presumably pro-American consensus, there is evidence of an unstable and unsettled public opinion. In the same vein, one can contrast the strong 61.3 percent that attributes the U.S. motivation to a goal of stopping terrorism (rather than some less-than-ideal ulterior motive) with the 43.5 percent that negatively assess the American war in Afghanistan, describing U.S. humanitarian aid as "useless, hypocritical or insincere." In sum, the German press accounts of America in the context of September 11 reflect a slight predisposition to support the American initiative in the war against terrorism while also revealing considerable hesitation just below the surface.

The final pertinent data from this study involve descriptions of the United States. Initially the findings seem unexciting: the only term that gets a significant percentage of hits is the obvious designation of the United States as "the only superpower" at 20.1 percent. Nearly all the many other terms get low ratings. Nonetheless, explicitly negative characterizations total 13.4 percent, which is hardly insignificant. These terms include designations such as indifferent, stupid, exploitable, naïve, money-hungry, "capitalism in a negative sense," warlike, and terrorists. These data also corroborate the overall profile presented by the content analysis data. The hypothesis of universal solidarity with the United States in the months immediately following the September 11 attack is not borne out by the evidence. Although German press representations of the United States in this period are somewhat positive or pro-American, there are indications of instability in the structure of public opinion and, depending on the particular question, considerable hostility as well. This negative potential, recorded here in the contents of the print media, could come to play a larger role during the following eighteen months, as the German political leadership positioned itself against the United States, and the United States proceeded from the war on terrorism in Afghanistan to the less obvious and more consequential case of regime change in Iraq.

Worldviews 2002

The textured account of the German press representations of the United States in the fall of 2001 is corroborated in various ways by the findings of the public opinion survey sponsored by the Chicago Council on Foreign Relations and the German Marshall Fund in June of 2002.[3] A pro-American predisposition and sets of shared values coexist with hesitation, opposition, and elements of anti-Americanism.

It is certainly true that with regard to many issues, public opinion in Germany and the United States is similar. This is hardly surprising: both countries are advanced industrial societies with stable democratic regimes, similarities that only amplify long histories of cultural interaction, from extensive German emigration to the United States in the nineteenth century to the American occupation in West Germany after the Second World War. Despite the hostile world-war experiences themselves, extensive exchange and positive interaction have also characterized the German-American relationship. Indeed, in the early 1990s it seemed possible that Germany might even become the primary anchor of the trans-Atlantic relationship, perhaps even displacing the special relationship between the United States and the United Kingdom. Of course, against this not-so-distant past of exceptionally strong German-American relations, the precipitous deterioration of German-American relations since September 11 is all the more remarkable.

The proof of shared values in Germany and the United States—like the evidence of extensive support for the United States in the German press after September 11—is pronounced. Seventy-three percent of Germans and 75 percent of Americans support expanded education spending. Similarly, 67 percent of Germans support greater programs to combat violence and crime, as compared with 70 percent of Americans. In both cases,

---

3. Chicago Council on Foreign Relations, *Worldviews 2002: Comparing American and European Public Opinion on Foreign Policy* (Chicago Council on Foreign Relations, 2002). http://www.worldviews.org.

the differences are negligible; public values are similar in the two countries. There is also considerable overlap in the estimation of world problems. Fifty-five percent of Germans see Islamic fundamentalism as a possible threat to their vital national interests, as compared with 61 percent of Americans. Forty-seven percent of Germans view global warming as extremely important, effectively identical with 46 percent of Americans.

This sort of evidence can be cited to show the continuing vitality of a community of values, the shared perspectives in Germany and the United States, which can then be taken as demonstrating the fundamentally solid relationship between the two countries. Yet this reassuring conclusion would not only ignore the real character of German-American relations between September 11 and the Iraq war. It would also ignore the public opinion data that demonstrate the basis for tension. As will be discussed later, there are plenty of policy points where Germans and Americans do not see eye to eye. In other words, the political conflict between Germany and the United States cannot be attributed only to diplomatic failures or deleterious personal interactions between the respective political leaders. Rather the *Worldviews 2002* survey, examined closely, yields evidence of an anti-American potential in German public opinion, which was foreshadowed in the content analysis of German print media after September 11.

A crucial issue involves attitudes toward future defense spending. In both Germany and the United States 38 percent of those surveyed believe that defense spending should not change, but that is as far as the similarity goes on this point. Otherwise the data are diametrically opposed. In the United States, 44 percent support expanded defense spending, and 15 percent call for cutbacks; in Germany, 45 percent urge cutbacks, and only 14 percent argue for expanding the defense budget. The distinctiveness of the German position can be better understood if it is compared with the aggregate European findings as well as with those of other individual European countries. For Europe in general, there is 22 percent support for expanded defense spending and 33 percent support for less (i.e., Germans are not only less supportive of defense spending than are Americans, but they are less supportive of defense spending than is Europe as a whole). Only the Netherlands (6 percent) and Italy (12 percent) have lower rates for supporting increased defense spending.

The pronounced antimilitary sentiment in Germany is an effect of German national history, the defeat in two world wars, the extraordinary devastation—physical and moral—associated with the Second World War, and the habit acquired during the cold war of relying on American military protection. That national history structures public opinion on this point is confirmed by the findings for other European countries. The German ratio for expanding and cutting back defense spending, 14:45 (percentages of the polled public supporting expansion and reduction), is closest to the Italian results of 12:52. (The results for the Netherlands are anomalous because of a curiously high rate for making no change and keeping defense spending at the same level.) In contrast, the two primary American allies in the world wars display slight majorities for increased spending: in the United Kingdom 24 percent for expanded spending and 21 percent for cutbacks, and in France 28 percent for expansion and 23 percent for cutbacks. Whether a country was on the winning or the losing side in the Second World War evidently has a significant effect on attitudes toward defense spending.

The findings for Poland are particularly noteworthy with

percentages nearly identical to the findings for the United States: 45 percent for expanded spending and 14 percent for cutting back (indeed, if only by a 1 percent difference, Polish public opinion supports increased defense spending more adamantly than does American). It is worthwhile to note that these findings predate the "old Europe versus new Europe" controversy, but they lend considerable credence to the hypothesis. The German public views defense spending in the light of a catastrophic militaristic history; Polish public opinion addresses the question in the light of a long history of threatened independence and a need to be able to defend its territorial integrity and sovereignty.

When asked to comment on whether the United States should exert strong leadership in world affairs, the aggregate findings for Europe show 31 percent viewing such an outcome as undesirable (22 percent as somewhat undesirable and 9 percent as very undesirable). The German total is 27 percent (i.e., a somewhat less negative view of American leadership than in Europe as a whole, although considerably above the American response at 14 percent). The combined negative results for France total 48 percent. With regard to hostility to American leadership in world affairs, there is therefore a significant anti-American minority in Germany, but it is less significant in scope than in Europe as a whole and considerably smaller than in France.

German attitudes to the United States, however, are not only the function of direct estimations of U.S. policy, past or future. They are also consequences of how Germans evaluate the European Union (EU) and their own role in world affairs. Question 7 of the *Worldviews 2002* survey asks whether it is desirable for the EU to exert strong leadership. Twenty-seven percent of Germans saw a leadership role for the EU as very desirable. Interestingly, this is the lowest rate for any European country (except Poland, at 16 percent, which at that time was not in the EU). Even in the United States, more Americans saw a leadership role for the EU as desirable (31 percent) than did Germans. The findings were 32 percent in the United Kingdom, 40 percent in France, 42 percent in the Netherlands, and 53 percent in Italy. The Germans appear to be the least supportive of EU leadership. Yet Question 9, asking whether one's own country should play an active role in world affairs, again found Germans least willing to be engaged. Although it is true that a majority of 65 percent stated that Germany should be active in world matters, that rate is far below the aggregate European findings of 78 percent and positively overshadowed by 82 percent in the United Kingdom, 86 percent in France, and even 90 percent in Italy. In both cases, the German findings indicate a greater hesitation, on the European and the national level, to take on prominent responsibilities in world affairs. It is plausible to argue that, as with defense spending, the German national past restrains the German public from articulating an aspiration for leadership in international matters.

This result is confirmed by another German anomaly. Sixty-five percent of Europeans support the notion that the EU should become a superpower like the United States. In Italy the rate soars to 76 percent and in France to 91 percent. The finding for Germany is a humble 48 percent, the only finding below 50 percent for any European country. As in the above examples, Germans display a cautious predisposition to avoid exposure in world affairs. Yet among those Europeans who do support superpower status for the EU, there is considerable variation in their vision for a future relationship with the United States. Although most respondents in all countries favor cooperation with the United States over competition, the findings for Germany indicate a significantly more competitive, and therefore less cooperative, relationship with the United States than is expressed by the public elsewhere in Europe. Eleven percent of Europeans favor a competitive relationship with the United States: the figure for Germany is 22 percent, as compared with France at 9 percent, the United Kingdom at 7 percent, and Italy at 5 percent. Meanwhile cooperation is favored by 84 percent of Europeans in general, 87 percent of the French, 89 percent of the British, 92 percent of the Italians, but only 70 percent of the Germans. Clearly, even in Germany, the proponents of cooperation are more numerous than are the proponents of competition. Nonetheless, Germany tilts toward a more adversarial posture to the United States in a way that distinguishes it from its European neighbors. This finding confirms the observation in the print media content analyses of a significant minority predisposition toward anti-American positions.

Still, the data leave us with a seemingly paradoxical finding: a German public opinion that, in response to several questions, displayed a greater hesitation toward world affairs than was characteristic of other European nations, yet at the same time evidence of a possibly greater adversarial stance toward the United States than displayed elsewhere in Europe. Both attitudes can, of course, be explained by the internal factors of German national history: the scars of earlier German international ambitions on the one hand, and on the other, resentment against the United States, the erstwhile opponent. This profile also maps onto the cultural-historical model of a romantic "German interiority": an inward-turning rejection of the world, coupled with an imperious external projection. As tempting as the thesis might be, however, the data at hand are insufficient to prove it. The two positions at stake—international hesitation and competition with the United States—are not conclusively linked (i.e., the findings may well derive from separate sectors of the public). One can conjecture, for example, that the greater reluctance to engage in international matters, reflecting the German past, might be associated with older generations, and the adversarial relationship to the United States might plausibly derive from the ideological background of the population in the new states (i.e. the formerly Communist East Germany). More differentiated data would be needed to explore these hypotheses.

Views of a Changing World, June 2003

While a "German interiority" hypothesis is not conclusively supported by the data, nothing disproves it either. Greater demographic differentiation of the data would be helpful, for example, in order to distinguish among the attitudes of various population sectors. Nonetheless certain conclusions are possible. The content analysis identified a preponderance of pro-American descriptors in the immediate aftermath of September 11; part of that support may represent a September 11 solidarity effect, but surely some indicates older pro-American sympathies in parts of the German public. Yet any solidarity effect related to the September 11 attacks was, as we have seen, clearly not universal. Therefore, it appears that the later deterioration of German-American relations cannot be attributed to some failure to make the American case in the German press. On the contrary, that case was being made from September 2001 on. The point is rather that support for the United States was never universal; other political positions were also present in the public debate, and this debate reflected deep fissures in German attitudes regarding world affairs. In other words, internal factors—German history, cultural values, and the structure of public debate—have evidently played crucial roles in formulating German attitudes toward the United States, including anti-American sentiments.

The Pew Global Attitudes Project survey, *Views of a Changing World, June 2003*, provides insights that allow us to trace the problem of Germany and the United States out another year. The image of the United States throughout Europe dipped in the course of the Afghanistan and Iraq wars, but by June of 2003 it rebounded, although not to the levels of 1999/2000. Nowhere has this trajectory been as precipitous as in Germany: from a 78 percent favorable image of the United States in 1999/2000 to 61 percent in the summer of 2002 (Schroeder election campaign) to 25 percent in March of 2003 (Iraq war) and then to 45 percent in June 2003. The difference between the extensive support for the United States at the outset to the June 2003 standing of 45 percent—in other words, less than half of Germans having a positive image of the United States— is a measure of the dramatic decline in German-American relations. These data also shed light on the question of the internal-external formulation of attitudes toward the United States. The fact that similarly curved trajectories are observable in other European countries indicates that any adequate explanation cannot be restricted to endogenous German circumstances alone. External factors are clearly at stake (i.e., the character of United States policy and the European, rather than merely German, perspective). Yet the fact that the German curve is so extreme is a result of internal German cultural factors: the pro-American legacy of cold war era relations on the one hand, and on the other, the devastating judgment on the American wars viewed through the historically over-determined lens of German pacifism. The positive approval rate for the United States in Germany has dropped by a remarkable 33 percentage points, more than it has dropped anywhere else. (The rate in France has gone from 62

percent to 43 percent, a loss of only 19 points; in Italy, from 76
percent to 60 percent, a loss of 16 points; and in Russia, from
37 percent to 36 percent, a loss of just 1 point.)[4]

It is not unreasonable to assume that estimations of another
country are based partly on perceptions of value systems: shared
values may support a positive estimation, whereas conflicting
values may lead to negative judgments. In this case, it is worthwhile to differentiate among various constellations: German
congruence with American values because of a shared "western"
paradigm; differences between America and Europe, including
Germany; differences within Europe; and so forth. The Pew
study provides examples of some of the possible permutations.
Evaluating the statement "Most people are better off in a free
market economy, even though some people are rich and some
are poor," 72 percent of Americans said they would completely
agree or mostly agree. The finding for Germany is 69 percent,
although in West Germany the finding is identical with that of
the United States, at 72 percent. Findings in other Western
European countries vary minimally: United Kingdom, 66 percent; France, 61 percent; Italy, 71 percent. Interestingly, the free
market finds considerably less approval in Eastern Europe:
Poland at 44 percent; Russia at 45 percent; and Bulgaria at 31
percent. (The most westernized part of Eastern Europe, the
Czech Republic, however, shows 62 percent support for the free
market, higher than in France.) In general, then, Western
Europe appears closer to the United States on the question of
the free market than does Eastern Europe, and Germany is the
country most like the United States.[5]

    4. Pew Global Attitudes Project, *Views of a Changing World, June 2003*
(Washington, D.C.: Pew Research Center for the People and the Press), 19.
    5. Ibid., T-6.

Yet when the statement is replaced with one regarding individual freedom and the force of social conditions, the findings change significantly. Evaluating the statement "Success in life is pretty much determined by forces outside our control," 32 percent of Americans completely or mostly agreed. The German finding is quite different, with 68 percent asserting the power of uncontrollable social forces (i.e., the opposite of individual initiative). This finding is at the high end of comparable Western European findings: the United Kingdom at 58 percent, France at 54 percent, Italy at 66 percent. Several of the Eastern European findings are surprisingly lower than those from Western Europe, that is, closer to the American data, although still much higher: Bulgaria at 52 percent, the Czech Republic at 47 percent, the Slovak Republic at 49 percent, but Poland at 63 percent (higher than many Western European countries but still lower than Germany). To the extent that, in the aggregate, the Eastern European findings are closer to the American, one finds a corroboration of an aspect of the "new Europe" thesis: the formerly Communist countries discovering an affinity with the United States that divides them, even in values orientation, from parts of Western Europe.[6] In any case, Germany is least like the United States on this point: where Americans trust individual initiative, Germans look to the power of larger social forces.

One final variant on the same subject matter shuffles the deck again. Asked to choose between two desiderata, 58 percent of Americans chose to be "free to pursue goals without interference from the state" as opposed to 34 percent who opted for a "state guarantee that nobody is in need." No other advanced industrial country displays as stark a profile. Comparing only the "state guarantee," which received 34 percent in the

6. Ibid., T-7.

United States, the United Kingdom measures 62 percent, France 62 percent, Italy 71 percent, and Germany 57 percent.[7] If one looks only at West Germany (in other words, if one excludes the post-Communist effect from East Germany), the finding is lower, at 52 percent. Interestingly, the Germans are in a liminal position: very much within the European range on this question, with a preference for state intervention, but at the American, more individualistic, end of the spectrum. Arguably, the severe decline of the positive American image in Germany is a result of this particular values structure: Germans are, in some ways, most like Americans, at least within the Western European group, and therefore they are most susceptible not only to identification but also to disappointment. Although they are the Europeans closest to the American apprehension regarding an intrusive state, they are also furthest from Americans in their deterministic estimation of the power of social conditions over individual initiative. Skepticism of a strong state (presumably a legacy of the Nazi experience) coexists, counterintuitively, with much less of an individualistic ethos. The combination suggests a characteristically German orientation toward conservative stability, implying potential discomfort with the dynamic changes sometimes associated with the United States and American society.

Conclusions

The various data suggest a complex German perception of the United States, resulting from a long and intricate history. As soon as one concedes that different nations may respond to the United States differently, one has to recognize the role of local cultures and therefore of internal factors. It is hardly surprising

---

7. Ibid., T-42.

that fragments of the long German-American history resurface
to shape the cultural context within which contemporary American policy and actions are judged.

The complexity of German-American relations explains the
fragmented findings in the print media data survey: the strong
clustering of support for and opposition to U.S. initiatives. This
bipolarity explains a curious aspect of the debate about German
attitudes to the United States: assertions of anti-Americanism
typically elicit denials and demonstrations of extensive appreci-
ation for the United States. The distinctiveness of the German
case is that anti-Americanism and philo-Americanism exist side
by side. As much as Germany as a whole shares many American
values, it could also nurture the antiwestern and anti-American
subculture where the September 11 conspiracy germinated.

The data unfortunately lack the demographic precision that
would allow more specific attribution of anti-American attitudes
(e.g., on the basis of age, gender, income, education, or region).
Nonetheless, the negative characterizations in the print media
and some of the value conflicts allow a tentative inventory of the
types of anti-Americanism. The association of Americans with
"capitalism in a negative sense" in the context of the hesitations
regarding individualism indicates that an older, culturally conservative set of anxieties regarding the dynamism of capitalism
and democracy may be lingering as part of Germany's cultural
heritage. This predemocratic anti-Americanism finds expression
in contempt for aspects of American mass culture. In contrast,
there is surely a separate Communist anti-Americanism, inherited from the ideological inculcations of East Germany: hence
the attacks on American imperialism and the predisposition to
denounce the wars in Afghanistan and Iraq simply as continui-
ties of the U.S. history of interventions in the third world during
the cold war: Iraq as Vietnam, and so forth. Finally, a postde-

mocratic anti-Americanism has emerged (i.e., an anti-Americanism driven by the resentment that the United States has been
unwilling to cede sovereignty to the structures of international
governance, as European states have done in the process of
European unification). This difference has grown into an enormous conflict between the United States and the European
Union. Considerable hostility to the United States is in fact
fueled by the tenacity with which the American government has
resisted such internationalization and insisted on the priority of
national democratic processes. That this "unilateralism" is so irk-
some to Germany only reflects the passion with which German
politicians have been eager to pursue a postnational form of
government. To the extent, however, that democratic legitima-
tion still takes place largely on national (if not regional and
local) levels, resentment develops in response to this loss of sovereignty. American resistance to this tendency fans the flames all
the more. Whether, and in what ways, these three hypothetical
models map onto aspects of public opinion remains to be studied. How they inform the ideological life of anti-Americanism is
discussed in the next chapter.

2

Not Just a Friendly Disagreement
Anti-Americanism as Obsession

For a brief moment after the fall of the Berlin wall, anti-Americanism seemed to have disappeared, especially in Germany, where decades of American foreign policy—the airlift, Kennedy in Berlin, Reagan's call to tear down the wall—culminated in a clear victory. In fact, that triumph cast a glow far beyond Germany as well. The Soviet Union, the overriding opponent in one of the defining conflicts of the last century, had been defeated. America and the values of liberal democracy and neoliberal capitalism were the undisputed winners. The Left, the traditional locus of most anti-Americanism, was in disarray. The only remaining opponents were on the far Right, isolated European ideologues of anti-American anticapitalism.

Yet the moment was brief, ending quickly with the onset of the 1991 Gulf war, which elicited a widespread peace movement, notably in Germany, which treated the American-led international coalition against Iraq as an expression of a malicious imperialist design, rather than as a response to the Iraqi occupation of Kuwait.[1] Although it was indeed a new historical

1. See Russell A. Berman, "The Gulf War and Cultural Theory in the United States and Germany: Nationhood, Popularity and Yellow Ribbons," in Berman, *Cultural Studies of Modern Germany: History, Representation, and Nationhood* (Madison: University of Wisconsin Press, 1993), 175–200.

epoch—the cold war had ended, and with it the Soviet inspiration for anti-American propaganda—an anti-American political subculture continued to flourish. In fact, that hostility grew throughout the course of the decade, providing the defining framework for European debates around an ever-shifting set of topical concerns: the Israeli-Palestinian conflict, the anxieties regarding globalization, international economic relations, and the efforts to develop an international agenda for ecological concerns, which came to be associated with the negotiations in Kyoto. No matter how the specific topic migrated, a discursive framework remained constant, always casting America as the fundamental source of discord. This analytic predisposition was nowhere more common than in Germany. While the terrorist attacks of September 11, 2001, produced a momentary solidarity effect with the United States, they did not significantly mitigate the anti-Americanism that grew widespread in the Western European public.

In fact, it was precisely that vigorous anti-American subculture that made Germany such a hospitable venue for Mohammed Atta and his terrorist partners as they prepared for the attacks on Washington, D.C., and New York. Yet, far from recognizing the European responsibility for having nurtured, harbored, and funded terrorists and terrorist networks, anti-Americans turn matters on their head, grotesquely blaming the United States for 9/11. For anti-Americans, especially in Europe, the United States is always guilty, even when it is the victim. Logic ceases to matter, allowing for mutually exclusive accusations. For example, while some anti-Americans suggest that terrorists carried out 9/11 in response to the alleged provocations of American foreign policy (suggesting that the attacks were a necessary consequence of U.S. policy), others insinuate that it was the Americans themselves who had engaged in a secret plot to attack the Pentagon and the World Trade Center in order to gain political advantage by acting as agents provocateurs. This conspiracy theory proposition is of course outrageous, but—like most extremist propositions—it is ultimately undisprovable to those who enjoy indulging in such fantasies and who are always willing to believe the worst and most macabre claims about the U.S. government. However, the former position, interpreting the attacks as a plausible response to American foreign policy, is equally obnoxious because it is intended as an implicit justification for terror. As will be discussed later, there may well be a relationship between the attacks—standing now as the supreme expression of anti-Americanism—and aspects of U.S. policy, but in a very different sense from the anti-American claim that U.S. policy is the ultimate cause. For now, however, suffice it to say that anti-Americanism has become an important factor in contemporary political life, in Germany and elsewhere in Europe—despite the end of Communism and despite the scope of the terrorist threat. Hence the urgency of posing the question: Where does anti-Americanism come from?

It is a frequent misunderstanding to treat the term "anti-Americanism" as a designation for any opposition to a particular policy of the U.S. government or to the influence of American society and culture. If that broad definition were to apply, then reasonable critics of policy matters or cultural influence would fit the bill. Such an expansive definition renders the term useless. Not every opponent of American tax policy, for example, or every critic of American films is necessarily "anti-American." Anti-Americanism has nothing to do with friendly disputes or reasonable disagreements. Instead, as French author Jean-François Revel has put it, it is an "obsession."[2] Anti-Americanism is indicated precisely when reasoned argument gives way to sweeping generalizations and hostile innuendo, and the obsessive thought structures of prejudice and stereotype prevail. Although a particular policy dispute may serve as a pretext, anti-Americanism is driven by a deeper and more expansive fixation on an image or idea of America, burdened with multiple negative associations that extend far beyond a bone of contention about any particular policy.

If a European dislikes jazz, that does not make him anti-American. It is only a matter of musical taste. However, if the dislike is embedded in a racist dismissal of African-Americans, then it does become a matter of anti-Americanism: prejudicial obsession has displaced a possible musical discussion. Similar distinctions apply in foreign policy matters. Criticism of American policy in Iraq is, in and of itself, not anti-American, but when—as was the case in Germany—that criticism is accompanied by a general dismissal of "American conditions," one has to recognize that anti-Americanism has come into play. A useful test is refutability: in a policy debate on Iraq, one can imagine attempting to rebut critics who present a specific rationale, but it is impossible to mount a meaningfully argued reply to irrational prejudice.

Anti-Americanism functions like a prejudice, magnifying the power and presence of its presumed opponent, turning it into a ubiquitous threat. The empirical superiority of American military power, for example, is transformed by the anti-American imagination into a fantasy of infinite omnipotence: there is no evil in the world that cannot be blamed on American action, if

2. Jean-François Revel, *L'obsession anti-américaine: Son fonctionnement, ses causes, ses consequences* (Paris: Plon, 2002).

only because the one superpower did not choose to stop it. Why should American humanitarian motives be believed in any single case if Americans have failed to pursue them in all possible cases? Because America is assumed to have unlimited power, it can be given unlimited blame. Any event in the world can therefore be attributed to the machinations of American conspiracy.

This structure of thinking is comparable to other political fantasies. At the height of the cold war, the core supporters of Joseph McCarthy interpreted all the events around them in terms of an allegedly perfectly functioning Communist conspiracy. Antisemites, similarly, have always been able to imagine an ineluctable network of Jewish power. As a paranoid fantasy, anti-Americanism is cut from the same cloth. Instead of facing up to the detailed complexity of reality, it can only see Washington's hand controlling every conflict. The point is not that the United States is weak—on the contrary, it is indisputably the one superpower—but the United States is not, indeed can never be, as infinitely strong as the anti-American true believer imagines. This disjunction between American reality and the anti-American fantasy is symptomatic. The character of prejudice is such that it ultimately has very little to do with the reality of its object. Yet while the discourse of anti-Americanism has little to do with American reality, it does reveal the character and mentality of anti-American Europe.

This leads to the central claim in this chapter: anti-Americanism is not a response to American policies, American influence, or any broader process of "Americanization." The anti-American may of course point to an allegedly ubiquitous American presence in order to legitimate a hostile response: because American power is allegedly unlimited, America must be opposed everywhere. Yet this insinuated causality is ultimately not plausible. Anti-Americanism has a secret life of its own. It cannot be correlated to specific instances of American presence: hence the proposition that anti-Americanism is largely independent of American policy or presence (or Americanization). Anti-Americanism is not a rational response to American action; rather, the fantasy of infinite American presence is a product of the anti-American's heated imagination.

The assertion that anti-Americanism is not the effect for which American action was the cause can be demonstrated in several ways. Although anti-Americanism is surely only a minority position in all national populations, one can find evidence of anti-Americanism in many different settings: in countries with histories of a considerable American presence (like Germany) as well as in countries with very different histories of involvement with the United States (like France). Yet since a comparable (if not fully identical) anti-Americanism colors political culture in those two countries, then clearly the history of occupation and Americanization in Germany—a history that France does not share—is not a pertinent variable. Western European anti-Americanism takes place in countries with very different degrees of Americanization and therefore very different experiences of American reality. The fact that anti-Americanism can appear in countries whose encounters with the United States have been radically different from each other shows that anti-Americanism is not the function of a real-world experience of the United States or of American behavior. Far from a reasonable response to real-world situations, it is a political fantasy, an irrational, ideological view of the world that spreads largely independently of any objective contact with the United States or its culture.

With regard to Germany, the key country in the process of European unification, three further observations bolster the claim that anti-Americanism is not explicable as an effect of American action. First, to the extent that American policy serves as a pretext for anti-Americanism, a curiously selective vision applies. Currently, at least, German anti-Americanism refers to American foreign policy, particularly in Iraq, but then it is surely odd that the elements of American foreign policy most relevant to Germany—such as the support for German unification, against the implicit resistance of France and England—have dropped out of the discussion.[3] If anti-Americanism were genuinely a response to American policies, then one would expect that American policy toward Germany would also figure in the German discussion, and not merely American policy toward Iraq. Of course, one can assume that an underlying resentment of German unification and nostalgia for the Communist regime of East Germany may fuel some of the anti-Americanism, at least in the circles of the former Communist Party (the PDS). In this case, the paradox of German anti-Americanism would be no paradox at all but merely a lingering effect of the cold war. Yet although there is surely an element of this Communist effect in the post-Communist world, it is only part of the larger phenomenon, which requires a more comprehensive account: German anti-Americanism includes a Communist element but clearly extends far beyond the Communist camp and cannot be adequately explained as a desire to resurrect the East German regime. In any case, the fact that it is American foreign policy that is under attack, whereas American foreign policy in relation to Germany is excluded from the discussion, demonstrates that anti-Americanism does not represent a rational response to policy. On the contrary, it is about fantasy and ideology: anti-Americanism, while taking the United States as a pretext, in fact

3. Philip Zelikow and Condoleezza Rice, *Germany Unified and Europe Transformed: A Study in Statecraft* (Cambridge: Harvard University Press, 1995).

expresses some other displaced anger. It is evidently not American actions that elicit the hostile sentiment.

Second, the lack of a causal connection between American presence and anti-Americanism is evidenced in Germany insofar as anti-Americanism has increased precisely as the American military presence in Germany has decreased, in the wake of unification. The willingness of leading German public figures to engage in hostile characterizations of the United States is greater, even though there are fewer Americans around and there is presumably less American influence. When American troops were at full strength, no German Chancellor would have campaigned with anti-American rhetoric, and no German minister would have compared an American president to Hitler. It is hard to avoid the speculation that a certain German nationalist rhetoric only became possible once American troop size declined. Now that American troops are no longer necessary to face down the Soviet military in Central Europe, there is less reason to refrain from making political capital out of anti-American rhetoric.

Yet it is not even necessary to make the strong case: greater anti-Americanism in the context of less American presence. To show the lack of a causal relationship between American action and anti-American sentiment, it is sufficient to point out that the enormous reduction of American troop size has simply not led to a corollary reduction in anti-Americanism. For example, during the "peace movement" of the 1980s involving the NATO double-track decision and the stationing of the Pershing missiles, much to-do was made of presumed restrictions imposed on West German sovereignty because of the postwar power relations and the dependence on the United States. A certain hostility to America followed, or was imagined to follow, from that situation; it was argued that the post-1945 limitation on West

German sovereignty imposed by the victorious United States was grounds for anti-American feeling. With the unification of Germany, that restriction on German sovereignty disappeared; nonetheless, a similar hostility continues to be directed at the United States. Thus the claim made during the 1980s that anti-Americanism was due to the perceived restriction of German sovereignty by American power on the basis of post–Second World War arrangements is obviously not tenable. Even though Germany regained its full sovereignty and the alleged grounds for anti-American sentiment disappeared, anti-Americanism continued to thrive. This is further evidence that German anti-Americanism has nothing to do with these aspects of German-American relations. Indeed anti-Americanism appears to be independent of the real character of these relations altogether. It is this lack of connection to reality that makes it a matter of ideology. Yet ideologies and fantasies can have very real impact on the substance of politics.

It is, however, a third observation that clinches the argument, demonstrating the independence of anti-Americanism from American actions. Not only is anti-Americanism found in contexts where no significant Americanization (or occupation) has taken place; not only does anti-Americanism evidently postdate the decline of an American presence in Germany; but in fact, anti-Americanism long predates the post–Second World War occupation and anything that might properly be described as Americanization. Anti-Americanism is not a response to particular actions or deeds but a cultural mentality that, emerging long before the rise of American power in the early twentieth century, is a reaction against the very presence of America in the world. The European discovery of the new world upset the traditional European worldview, with Europe self-confidently at the center. Indeed, ever since the so-called first contact of European travelers with the inhabitants of the new world, Europeans have expressed anxieties regarding the brute nature, the presumed absence of history, and an undifferentiated homogeneity imputed to the western hemisphere.[4] These are precisely the standard tropes of anti-Americanism, an ideology with a long past, replete with stereotypes that are regularly recycled in new historical circumstances.

A German discourse of anti-Americanism became prominent, at the latest, in the early nineteenth century as romantic authors like the poet Nikolaus Lenau increasingly described the United States in pejorative terms, associated with their negative judgments on both its capitalism and its democracy. In contrast, the towering German author of the age, Johann Wolfgang Goethe, repeatedly expressed admiration for the young American republic. His opposition to the romantic antimodern reaction indicates the initial phase of a positive German attraction to America and the values of modernity associated with the American Revolution.[5] The deep, competing currents of pro-American and anti-American perspectives in German culture, in other words, are quite old, which underscores why German anti-Americanism cannot be explained away as a friendly policy dispute or even as a response to aspects of the role the United States has played in Germany in the twentieth century. The terms of the anti-American discourse have been in circulation at least since the romantic early nineteenth century. Thus, it is not anything that the United States does to Germany, no recognizable Americanization, that elicits anti-Americanism. It is rather the

4. See Suzanne Zantop, *Colonial Fantasies: Conquest, Family, and Nation in Precolonial Germany, 1770–1870* (Durham: Duke University Press, 1997), 18–42.

5. Dan Diner, *America in the Eyes of the Germans: An Essay on Anti-Americanism,* trans. Allison Brown (Princeton: Markus Wiener, 1996), 37.

mere fact of the presence, in the world, of a society defined in terms of capitalism and democracy that scandalizes sectors of German and old European society. It is not an intrusive imposition of America's democratic capitalism that provokes the protests but the mere temptation that it represents.

This formulation, however, sheds a new light on the causation problem. To say that anti-Americanism is not caused by American policies and actions means two things: it is not a result of specific American actions or cultural transfers, and it is not primarily a response to the projection of a specifically American identity, national interest, and so on. However if anti-Americanism is decoupled from real policies and actions, it does not follow that it has nothing to do with real experience. On the contrary, anti-Americanism does indeed represent a response to genuine forces of historical change. What is at stake, however, is not the remaking of the world in the image of America—a possible working definition of "Americanization"—against which anti-Americans believe they offer resistance, but rather the historical development in modernity toward democratic capitalism, which during the twentieth century has transpired disproportionately through American power and influence. Anti-Americanism is, fundamentally, the rhetoric of opposition to this global historical process of political and economic emancipation. Pretending to oppose American power, anti-Americanism is in fact the ideology of opposition to the democratization of politics and the liberalization of markets.

It is in the nature of such political rhetoric that little value is placed on consistency. Like other obsessive ideologies, anti-Americanism is internally heterogeneous, and it draws on multiple cultural-historical currents. One can however distinguish heuristically among different registers of anti-Americanism, in particular the following three:

1. *Predemocratic anti-Americanism* expresses an aristocratic (or
   imitatively aristocratic) disdain for the life of democracy,
   deemed too ordinary, banal, and lacking in quality. America
   is taken to represent the driving force of modernization as
   trivialization; nostalgia for the golden age of a premodern
   world therefore turns into anti-Americanism. Although
   these attitudes may have resonated among the members of
   the traditional aristocracy, it is not that tiny social group
   that is important. Rather this version of anti-Americanism
   has turned into a widespread hostility particularly in cultural
   sectors. It has migrated largely into the arts, generating, for
   example, the notion of America as lacking in high culture.
   Anti-Americanism contrasts the allegedly low quality of
   American mass culture (Hollywood cinema) with presumably higher standards of quality in Europe; or more generally,
   it reduces the world to a simple opposition between American quantity and European quality.

2. *Communist anti-Americanism* emerged from the ideological
   apparatus of the Communist movement during the nearly
   seventy-five years between the Bolshevik seizure of power
   and the collapse of the Soviet Union. The global struggle
   between Russian interests, masked as Communist, and the
   democratic agenda of the free world under U.S. leadership
   structured much political and intellectual life for most of the
   past century. In the battle with twentieth-century totalitarianism, the United States sometimes entered into unholy alli-
   ances with undemocratic regimes; such is the complexity of
   politics. Just as the United States entered into a strategic alliance with Stalin to defeat Hitler, it had to back undemocratic regimes in the cold war struggle against Soviet power.
   Moreover, it should surprise no one that foreign policies,

like any government-generated practice, sometimes become internally inconsistent. The point is that inconsistencies such as these became targets for Communist propaganda and were taken as evidence of Western hypocrisy. Yet with the collapse of the Soviet empire, American foreign policy is gradually returning to its core values and to the predisposition to support governments that are democratic or moving toward democratization.[6] (Marx himself largely admired the dynamism of American capitalism and democracy and did not participate in the anti-Americanism that came to be the hallmark of Communist ideology in the twentieth century.)[7] Although the opening of the Berlin wall and the subsequent collapse of the Soviet empire has meant the real collapse of the apparatus of Communist propaganda, the discourse of Communist anti-Americanism remains in effect, particularly but not only in former Communist circles. Where predemocratic anti-Americanism typically turns into the cultural criticism of the United States, Communist anti-Americanism still focuses especially on foreign policy disputes from the cold war era: Vietnam, Cuba, Chile, Grenada, and so forth.

3. *Postdemocratic anti-Americanism* involves current complaints that the United States remains reluctant to surrender elements of its sovereignty in order to transfer them to international bodies. Advocates of forms of international governance oppose the American insistence on national independence as a precondition for the democratic expression of popular will. Whatever the standing of international governance bodies may be, they are in any case not elected

6. *The National Security Strategy of the United States*, September 2002, preface, n.p. (p. iii), http://whitehouse.gov.

7. Diner, *America in the Eyes of the Germans*, 46.

institutions. At best, one might say that they are institutions set up through treaties by several states; yet not only are many of those states barely democratic, if at all, but the very presumption that a state would significantly subordinate itself to the will of others in institutions with no external control runs counter to liberal democratic expectations. In addition, the prominence of nongovernmental organizations in contemporary international debate highlights a sensitive distinction between democratic sovereignty and private advocacy. Postdemocratic anti-Americanism involves the assertion of the will of the experts, organized in partisan advocacy associations, over the will of the people as expressed in electoral processes.

These three types of anti-Americanism can overlap and coexist within the same material. In fact, one finds all three variants in the German responses to September 11, which have been documented in a volume edited by the journalist Henryk Broder: a collection of revealing statements by German writers, intellectuals, and politicians. Because anti-Americanism is a cultural phenomenon, expressing historical predispositions, political fantasies, and irrational ideologies, it is appropriate that so much of the evidence derives from the cultural sector. This is particularly true for predemocratic anti-Americanism, typically associated with the aesthetic attitude of cultural elitism. This attitude is characterized by a typically strained effort to maintain composure and to foreground a cool, even cold, attitude, to suggest that the terrorist attacks were, ultimately, not very important. Representatives of this version of anti-Americanism attempt to demonstrate how they are simply too important to be concerned with the suffering of the day, the significance of which they denigrate. The goal of predemocratic anti-Americanism is to demonstrate a lack of concern, belying the myth of universal solidarity with victims. A good example is found in the comments of the award-winning and bestselling German author Martin Walser on his experience of September 11:

> I had to give a reading in Bamberg [on Sept. 11]. I asked myself whether it would really be appropriate to read from a novel called *The Life of Love*, but the organizer said we should proceed in any case. And then I gave into a whim and said [to the audience]: "The Americans are getting in my way again." The audience was irritated, so I explained that the premiere of my play *Larger than Life Mr. Krott* was scheduled for November 21, 1961 [*sic*], but it was cancelled due to the Kennedy assassination. Then I gave my reading, and afterwards two listeners said to me: "You helped us forget today's events." That was a wonderful experience for me as an author.[8]

Walser's point is to demonstrate a studied lack of sympathy by hiding behind aestheticism as an aristocratic posture. It is the work of art that counts, and not the count of the victims. The point is not the appropriateness of having proceeded with the reading on September 11 but Walser's dismissing the conflict as a humorous matter of American intrusiveness. For Walser, the importance of his literature obviously and unquestionably overshadows any interest in the human suffering of the attacks. The popular philosopher Peter Sloterdijk similarly dismisses the scope of the tragedy. With an *en passant* reference to the "catastrophe landscape" of the twentieth century, he diminishes September 11 to a "barely noticeable, minor accident"[9] Similarly, during the first weeks after the attack, when one thought the

---

8. Cited in Henryk M. Broder, *Kein Krieg, Nirgends: Die Deutschen und der Terror* (Berlin: Berlin Verlag, 2002), 93. The correct date for the Kennedy assassination is November 22, 1963.

9. Ibid., 10.

body count was considerably higher, a columnist of the *taz*, a popular left-of-center newspaper, eagerly trivialized the event: "as regrettable as the death of seven thousand people in New York may be, measured against what is taking place elsewhere in the world, it is in comparison just a bagatelle."[10] In all these examples, the scope of the American dead is denied through the appeal to something always greater: an easy rhetorical trick.

Aside from revealing a lack of human sympathy, this pseudo-aristocratic contempt for American suffering strikes one as political misery. Desperate to diminish the importance of September 11, these commentators blind themselves to the enormous political consequences of the attacks, especially the transformed relationship of the United States to the world. Not only do they remain untouched by the human loss; their ideology prevents them from recognizing that September 11 would most likely change American foreign policy profoundly, for it was hardly a trivial matter when the policy of preemptive attacks was subsequently adopted. The more German opinion makers minimized September 11, the more they contributed to the minimization of Germany's standing in future foreign policy arrangements, as became clear later in the context of the Iraq war. Yet this reduction in the importance of Germany is a consequence of a consistently wrong arithmetic in parts of the German public sphere: fifty dead in Jenin—the site of a pitched battle between the Israeli army and Palestinian terrorists in the spring of 2002—was denounced as a "massacre," while even seven thousand American dead would have been counted as a "bagatelle."

Communist anti-Americanism, the second variant, recycles motifs from cold war propaganda and redirects them, once

10. Ibid., 123.

again, toward the United States. While predemocratic, cultural anti-Americanism treats human suffering dismissively, Communist anti-Americanism denounces suffering but blames it exclusively on the United States and world capitalism. For example, a Party of Democratic Socialism leaflet distributed in Hamburg commented on the September 11 attacks with the slogan "What goes around comes around."[11] In other words, the terrorists were justified in repaying like with like, meaning that the Americans got what they deserved. More notoriously, another aspect of Communist vocabulary reappeared as well: the pathos of the anti-Hitler rhetoric, turned against the United States—in particular against George W. Bush. What the German minister of justice, Herta Daübler-Gmelin, said in her equation of Bush and Hitler was in fact not at all exceptional; one can encounter similar remarks frequently in Germany. A noteworthy instance involved a large banner held up during the demonstrations against Bush in Berlin in May 2002, with pictures of Hitler pointing to the burning Reichstag and of Bush in front of the crumbling World Trade Center. To make the identification complete, they share the same cartoon bubble of speech:

> This attack means that our nation must set out on a long march to war and forget the debilitating trust in civil liberties! But do not fear, my people, for this just fight will only add to our glory!! And although this attack seems to be made to order to make you forget my disputed seizure of power and to pave the way for blind obedience to my orders, I want to have you believe that my security forces had nothing to do with it. Thank you very much. See you later in Poland or Iraq, and then around the world!![12]

11. "So was kommt von so was." Ibid., 200.
12. *The Times of London*, May 23, 2002, p. 17.

The poster tells us little about Bush and Hitler but a good deal about the political culture that could tolerate this sort of distorted representation. For starters, of course, in a classic Communist manner, the antisemitic character of Hitler's rhetoric and National Socialism is simply expunged. In addition, the conspiracy theory innuendo that American security forces carried out the September 11 attack is clear. More generally, the equation of the legal systems in Nazi Germany and contemporary America is striking: either it means that the contemporary, post-Communist Germans imagine that Nazi Germany was basically like the United States, and therefore not all that bad; or it implies a grossly distorted view of the United States and the standing of civil liberties. Yet we know that the German justice minister herself had described the American legal system as "lousy." Thus Communist imagery structures anti-Americanism in two ways: in its denunciation of the historical American defense of democracy against Soviet expansion and in its characterization of capitalism, and especially the most developed capitalist society, the United States, as fascist through the association with Hitler.

Although the predemocratic and Communist variants of anti-Americanism represent residues of obsolete political formations—no matter how these ideologies retain a contemporary afterlife—postdemocratic anti-Americanism, the third model, reflects an emerging divide: on the one hand, the widespread predisposition, perhaps more in Germany than elsewhere, to shift decision making to supranational and therefore undemocratic units—the European Union, the United Nations, an international court—and on the other, the American insistence on the priority of national sovereignty as an expression of popular will. The process of sovereignty transfer corresponds both to the larger political and economic pressure toward globalization and, simultaneously, to the logic of bureaucratization: it is one more way to allow the deferral and dispersion of decision making. The fact that Germany buys into this process of sovereignty transfer with special enthusiasm reflects its own ambivalent relationship to its particularly catastrophic national past and its impaired self-esteem (although there is plenty of willingness to engage in symbolic self-assertion as long as the opponent is the United States).[13] Because Germany, in order to overcome its past, is eager to shift decision making responsibility to a supranational structure, it expects all other nations to similarly renounce their national independence and dissolve into international, ultimately global, governance structures.

In the responses to September 11, this postdemocratic perspective emerged in expressions of concern that U.S. policy inappropriately responds to domestic constituencies. The (surely not incorrect) perception that American foreign policy takes the opinion of the American electorate into account is the bone of contention. In other words, there is an underlying assumption in parts of the anti-American European public that policy, and in particular foreign policy, ought to be decoupled from democratic political discussion and decision making (i.e., diminishing the domestic public sphere). Because foreign policy has international ramifications, it should, so the strange-but-true argument goes, be separated from domestic democratic will formation and, presumably, be shifted to international governance structures shielded from local political sentiment. Apparently, American politicians should listen less to voters and more to nongovernmental organizations. Thus the influential public intellectual and cultural critic Klaus Theweleit wrote: "It is fre-

---

13. Cf. Tom W. Smith and Lars Jarkko, "National Pride in Cross-National Perspective," paper of the National Opinion Research Center (University of Chicago, April 2001), http://www.issp.org/paper.htm.

quently overlooked that Bush could only win the elections with votes from the Bible Belt, the votes of fundamentalist Americans, religious fanatics. . . . And then Bush does not understand when armed religious fanatics come back from other parts of the world."[14]

Leaving aside the bizarre analogy of culturally conservative Christians to armed terrorists, one notes Theweleit's implicit objection to the notion that this particular group, perhaps any particular group, should be able to participate in the electoral process. Does he mean that Christian voters should be disenfranchised? Yet if one assumes that fundamentalist Christians do indeed have the right to vote—a right that Theweleit seems to dispute—then one cannot object to the possibility that their votes might have consequences with political influence. The same objection recurs even more frequently with regard to the Jewish vote, evident in the tedious German paranoia regarding a "Jewish lobby" somehow mysteriously steering American foreign policy.[15] It is this antisemitic content that regularly lurks behind the standard complaint that U.S. Middle East policy is the function of domestic political concerns.

Yet the notion that domestic politics ought to be excluded from foreign policy can mean nothing else than decoupling foreign policy formation from the democratic process. The logical conclusion would entail separating foreign policy from democratic government and relocating it in an independent foundation of objective experts: an absurd option, to be sure—but not that far from various proposals for international governance. In any case, given this European suspicion of the U.S. system as

---

14. Broder, *Kein Krieg, Nirgends,* 186.
15. William Safire, "The German Problem," *New York Times,* September 19, 2002, A35.

excessively democratic because of its propensity to respond to domestic politics, it is only consistent that much European public opinion does not proceed from a basic solidarity with democratic states, particularly in the Middle East. In contrast, one of the important successes of current U.S. policy has been the ability to focus international attention on the urgency of democratization throughout that region.[16]

These three types of anti-Americanism may overlap and intermingle. Moreover they take on specific colorations in different national contexts. French anti-Americanism is more commonly marked by a cultural denigration of America; hence, for example, Jean Baudrillard's celebration of the September 11 terrorists as noble savages, living authentically, in contrast to what he chose to refer to dismissively the "banality" of American life.[17] (This material is discussed more closely in chapter 5). Meanwhile the geopolitical element in French discourse is typically more oriented toward inventing space for France to imagine remaining among the key global players, in contrast to German provincialism, eager to defer to Europe or the U.N.[18] In Germany, too, one can find cultural criticism and allegations about the low quality of American culture. Communist-inspired accounts of twentieth-century history are more common in Germany than in France (part of the East German legacy). More frequently, however, German anti-Americanism is haunted by

16. On the urgency of democratic reform in the Arab world, cf. Claire Nullis, "Report: Arab Economies Need Reform," *Washington Times*, September 8, 2002, regarding "Arab World Competitiveness Report" of the World Economic Forum.

17. Jean Baudrillard, "The Spirit of Terrorism," trans. Kathy Ackerman, *Telos* 121 (Fall 2001), 138; cf. Alain Minc, "Terrorism of the Spirit," trans. Kathy Ackerman, *Telos* 121 (Fall 2001), 143–45; and more generally, Philippe Roger, *L'ennemi américain: Généalogie de l'antiaméricanisme français* (Paris: Seuil, 2002).

18. Regarding provincialism, cf. Karl Heinz Bohrer, "Provinzialismus (II): ein Psychogramm," *Merkur* 45, no. 3 (March 1991), 255–61.

the anxieties of German national history: the desperate need to relativize the Nazi past by imagining that the United States, Israel, or both are equally criminal. Hence the long history of denouncing America's "everyday fascism" and—in the 9/11 discussions—the constant parallels suggested between the Allied bombings in the Second World War and the air war in Afghanistan: both, so the analogic argument goes, are wrong. In other words, lingering resentment about the U.S. role in the Second World War contaminates the German judgment on current foreign policy. Evidence of current American wrongdoing seems to provide Germans an absolution for their own past.

What then is the source of anti-Americanism? The first part of the answer is negative: anti-Americanism is not the result of specific processes of cultural or institutional transfer that could be construed to entail an "Americanization." Yet this does not mean that anti-Americanism is nothing more than a free-floating discourse, with no relationship to real historical processes. On the contrary—and this is the second part of the answer—anti-Americanism is, fundamentally, an expression of hostility to societies of democratic capitalism. This dynamic sort of social formation involves a set of institutions that developed particularly through the history of Western culture and its values, and it has flourished especially in the United States, which has defended this model in the hot and cold wars of the twentieth century. Yet democratic capitalism and its associated values are not narrowly American or even exclusively Western. On the contrary, as a social model, it exercises enormous attraction for populations around the world, one result of which is immigration, as well as the remarkable ability of immigrant groups to integrate with the U.S. polity quickly. Against cultural relativists, it is important to assert that democracy is not a parochial artifact of American culture but rather an objective potential of humanity, even if the United States has become its primary, if sometimes reluctant, vehicle.

Anti-Americanism is therefore not a response to specific policies or actions. It is not about the spread of jazz or youth culture; nor is it, fundamentally, about the bombing of Dresden, the proliferation of McDonald's franchises in Paris, or even the sanctions on Iraq, although each of these might be taken as a pretext and each, one can add, might well be debated on its own terms. Anti-Americanism, instead, involves a global judgment, an enormous stereotype, driven by fears regarding democracy and capitalism. The fact that the American model exercises such a magnetic attraction globally exacerbates the anxieties among those who do not emigrate and especially among national cultural elites, who resent their compatriots' opting for an American life-course. But this process, again, is not about the narrow assertion of American national interest or the particular contents of American culture. Nor is the key issue immigration, although the universal attraction of America—to peoples from very different cultural backgrounds—is quite telling and proof of the universal character of the specific set of values. The point is that the principles objectified in the American Revolution—products, to be sure, of particular cultural traditions—have proven to have universal appeal because they speak to basic aspects of the human condition everywhere. "Here or nowhere is America," spoke Goethe's Lothario in the novel *Wilhelm Meister's Apprenticeship*. By this he meant that the political and social revolution of democracy, initiated in the American Revolution, ought to be pursued in Germany, and not primarily through German emigration to the United States.[19] For Goethe, the structure of

19. Johann Wolfgang Goethe, *Goethes Werke*, ed. Erich Trunz (Hamburg: Christian Wegner Verlag, 1962), VII, 431.

emancipation—democratic government and free markets—
modeled in the United States was worthy of emulation elsewhere. It is that potential of freedom in human history that anti-
Americanism resists.

3 ✿
Democratic War, Repressive Peace
On Really Existing Anti-Americanism

Anti-Americanism in contemporary Europe has little to do with real policy disputes. Indeed, it has little to do with reality at all. On the contrary, it follows a topsy-turvy logic of obsessions driven by European fantasies about America. Drawing on long-standing cultural traditions rather than on contemporary conditions, anti-Americanism is trapped in a world of imagination. It is ideological in the sense that the ideals to which it adheres are never tested against hard facts. Chapter 2 explored how anti-Americanism is divorced from reality. This chapter discusses the consequence of this divorce: a political culture disconnected from the real world of facts and actions. In order to explore this aspect of anti-Americanism, it is necessary first to reflect on the standing of conflict in politics and culture. Against that background, this chapter proceeds to examine anti-Americanism's political instinct, its opposition to wars in the name of democracy, and its predisposition to maintaining the repressive peace of authoritarian regimes—the classical politics of appeasement. This political instinct has historical roots in the age of totalitarianism, but it is amplified, as will be shown, by the pursuit of an emerging European identity: the real voice behind the curtain of the anti-American Oz.

Conflict: Real and Imaginary

Politics typically involves conflicting interests, be it a matter of competition among individuals, parties, or states. The opposition of friend and foe in the international arena can grow into an enmity that takes the form of a dramatic scene, a confrontational face-off of two opponents. Accusation, recrimination, and attack unfold on the stage of doubled adversariness. It is doubled because the initial carrier of enmity, one side in the dispute, projects hostility on to the other, presuming that the opponent maintains a symmetrical counterview. The participant in the relationship of enmity assumes that the hostility is equally shared by the opponent. The drama of conflicting relations is therefore normally assumed to be a symmetrical arrangement.

Political theory offers alternative characterizations of conflict: either as an inescapable "state of nature," as an existential and irreducible struggle between irreconcilable foes, or as a precondition to an equally dramatic consensus-formation in a public sphere oriented toward compromise. The former model describes permanent war; the latter, the pursuit of a perpetual peace. As different as these outcomes are, the two alternatives and the gradations between them share an assumption: the substantiality of the opposition (i.e., the suggestion that a real, existence-defining conflict of interests underlies the hostility, whether the interests are religious or material, cultural or economic). In such a framework, enmity is understood to be the expression of conflict between genuine opponents. Real-world differences are presumed to be the underlying cause of political struggle.

Yet it is worth considering another sort of case, where conflict is not symmetrical in this sense and where prior or objective grounds are not the true cause of hostility. As was argued in chapter 2, anti-Americanism in fact follows its own ideological logic rather than genuinely conflicting interests. It is a cultural phenomenon rather than a rational pursuit of policy. When hostility results from such internal processes rather than from external conditions, the insinuation that the opponent is driven by symmetrical enmity amounts to little more than a fiction. By inventing the other as the enemy, one in fact ascribes to the other the sentiments that are above all one's own: I hate you so you must hate me. Yet in such a case, where the imputation of hostility is a fiction, the explanatory model of genuinely symmetrical enmity turns out to be wrong. It is now more a matter of an ideological strategy designed to justify hostility than an accurate description of an objective clash of interests. In contrast to the forms of hostility that result from a real-world interest conflict, other forms are the consequence of solely endogenous processes, all on one side of the conflict. This asymmetrical model requires an alternative explanation.

A primary anger in one party turns into anger at the world and only then finds its target. This hostility should be judged not as a response to what the opponent may have done, since the opponent is only a belated discovery. This sort of hostility, on the contrary, is an expression of an internal cultural or psychological process that requires the invention of a threat: an imagined enemy representing the fictive danger required to sustain a troubled identity. The image of the enemy is not the result of a real opposition but acts instead as a mechanism to confirm the identity of the group. The enemy, in this sense, is just a scapegoat, and the vilification of the scapegoat confirms the cohesion of the community. The discourse of enmity, the sharply contoured external-oriented narrative of hostility, turns out to be largely internally driven; rather than describing an external world, it plays a role in the construction of identity.

Hostility, in such cases, is not about the enemy but about the self. It involves an animus that predates the encounter with the presumed enemy. Instead of a model in which a real opponent elicits a hostile response, there is an internally generated anger, which only subsequently finds an object to oppose. This is the case for European anti-Americanism: it is not a matter of a plausible response to a real threat but rather the construction of an external enemy in order to maintain the coherence of an identity for Europe.

This argument concerning an endogenous or subjective hostility is not meant to pertain to all conflicts. In other cases, tragedy and opposition do exist and lead to real-world struggle. Here, however, it is a matter of conflicts that are primarily subjective, driven by the internal logic of a cultural or psychological need to find an opponent, rather than by a confrontation with a particular opponent in an objective competition for a specific good. In the case of a subjective hostility, the passion of belligerence, be it on the individual or collective level, is ultimately separate from and prior to the choice of the target of vilification. In political propaganda, this is precisely the dynamic that George Orwell described so masterfully in *1984*: mass sentiment would be channeled into hatred for ever-shifting opponents for reasons that had little to do with those opponents and everything to do with ensuring the stability of the totalitarian political culture. Hatred becomes a free-floating instinct, available for redirection toward whatever object is most expedient. The ritual denunciation of the opponent may refer to distant circumstances, but it serves a purpose closer to home. It has ultimately nothing to do with the vilified opponent's real existence, about which it prefers to remain largely ignorant and uninformed. Because it depends on this distance from and denial of facts, this sort of mind-set unleashes a continuing process of reality loss.

The drama of enmity is therefore false drama, as we can explore in the case of current European anti-Americanism.

The Case of Anti-Americanism

To say that European anti-Americanism lacks a genuinely dramatic scene means that it is not a reciprocal conflict between equal opponents. Anti-Americanism cannot be explained as part of a mirror-image hostility. There is, to be sure, some diffuse blowback, moments of anti-European hostility in the United States, but it is hardly ever on the scale of European anti-Americanism. The silly case of "freedom fries" is about as exciting as it gets: there are no anti-European demonstrations, no burnings of French or German flags, no angry mobs with pitchforks and tractors in front of Louis Vuitton boutiques or BMW dealerships. American "anti-Europeanism" is not an equal partner but only an anemic afterthought to the European spectacles.

Europe is hardly a matter of regular concern for the American public, whereas the United States represents an object of constant obsession for the anti-American mind: an omnipresent and omnipotent opponent. The asymmetry is evident in the imbalanced structure of transatlantic name-calling. Former French foreign minister Hubert Vedrine's complaint about the "simplistic" character of American foreign policy or German justice minister Herta Däubler-Gmelin's blunder equating Bush and Hitler generated irritation and bemused curiosity in America, but these remarks quickly became yesterday's news; in contrast, Donald Rumsfeld's comment on old and new Europe elicited outrage and vitriol. A raw nerve had been touched, and European intellectuals showed themselves eager to be provoked by an American secretary of defense. Facing that real enemy, the non-European, old grudges melted away, and Jacques Derrida and Jürgen Habermas, philosophers on two sides of the Rhine who have spent their careers attacking each other, promptly marched shoulder to shoulder against the perceived American threat. Where sober criticisms of Rumsfeld or American defense policy might have been plausible, the heavy hitters of the European spirit replied with the crude weapons of cultural denunciation and fantastic imagery that have characterized the anti-American mentality.[1]

Anti-Americanism is not a reasoned response to American policies; it is the hysterical surplus that goes beyond reason. That difference is evident in the constant recycling of anti-American images that have a history that long antedates current policy. The traditional European response to the new world and the United States has, for centuries, involved themes of savagery, violence, and excess power, as well as the anxieties generated by capitalism and democracy.[2] These stale images recur in the current discourse with stereotypical regularity. Yet if the animus predates the policy, then the policy is clearly not the cause but only the pretext, and the animus itself is prepolitical. Moreover, the obsessive mentality of anti-Americanism shows up in countries with very different experiences of the United States: Germany against the background of an occupation that was never perceived as a liberation (and certainly elicited no street celebrations), and France with the history of liberation but

1. Cf. Jürgen Habermas, et al., "Das alte Europa antwortet Herrn Rumsfeld," *Frankfurter Allgemeine Zeitung*, January 24, 2003, 33.

2. All this has been amply documented in various studies. Cf. Dan Diner, *America in the Eyes of the Germans: An Essay on Anti-Americanism*, trans. Allison Brown (Princeton: Markus Wiener, 1996); Philippe Roger, *L'ennemi americain: Généalogie de l'antiaméricanisme français* (Paris: Seuil, 2002); Susanne Zantop, *Colonial Fantasies: Conquest, Family, and Nation in Precolonial Germany, 1770–1870* (Durham: Duke University Press, 1997).

no occupation. Two different menus leave the same taste in the mouth, as if the flavor had a life of its own.

Yet this separation of the affect of enmity from hypothetically objective causes explains why the anti-American perception of the present is marked by the regular loss of factual grounding and a nearly hermetic imperviousness to events. Reality disappears. Hence the predisposition to disbelieve any reports of real American success in the Afghanistan or Iraq wars, to denounce pro-American Iraqis, and to exclude any information that does not fit into a narrowly constructed myth: "nothing can shake it in its inner certitude, because it is imprisoned in its safe world—because it is incapable of experiencing anything"— thus the literary critic Georg Lukács, writing nearly a century ago on the problem of "abstract idealism." His characterization precisely fits the substance of the anti-American mentality.[3] In this vein, one has to count the willingness of the mainstream European media to treat the Iraqi information minister as a plausible source, until the very end, while at the same time directing an unrelenting skepticism toward any signs of coalition victory or Iraqi celebrations. Because the anti-Saddam Iraqis disappointed the European anti-Americans, it was claimed that they did not exist or, at best, were funded by Americans. This sort of fantastic thinking with regard to the Iraq war, however, involves the very same reality denial that characterized another episode, the response to the September 11 attacks: the grotesque suggestions of hidden conspiracies or a mere media spectacle or—perhaps most common—the European notion that it was not that bad after all. Reality that does not match politically

3. Georg Lukács, *The Theory of the Novel: A Historico-Philosophical Essay on the Forms of Great Epic Literature*, trans. Anna Bostock (Cambridge: MIT Press, 1971), 99.

correct opinion cannot exist. Uncomfortable facts and uncomfortable opinions are equally disallowed. The sort of debate that has raged through the American public and press was just absent in much of Europe.

For anti-Americanism, the issue is not facts, to which one might respond critically, but an obsession, an internally generated hostility, with no link to the real world. Hence the predilection to denial: the Iraqis are not celebrating, Al Qaeda did not attack the Twin Towers, the infidels are not in Baghdad.

Because of this separation of ideology from reality, images take over, propagandistic targets of enmity, negatively charged icons. A telling case in point is the anti-American journalism of the Indian writer and activist Arundhati Roy. Obviously, Roy cannot be taken as an example of a typical European intellectual, but she has achieved a particular celebrity status in the European press, from the *Manchester Guardian* to the *Frankfurter Allgemeine*, which has published her anti-American essays. This prominence gives her writings a symptomatic significance (i.e., they can tell us something about the anti-American mentality).

Roy's style entails the rhetoric of antipathy, strings of stereotypical denunciations, devoid of reasoned argument and sprinkled with targets of hatred. It is, especially, a language that relies on derogatory personifications that serve to focus the reader's hatred. In one essay, for example, she arbitrarily conjures up an otherwise unidentified "marrowy American panelist," and in another she points with disgust at an equally anonymous figure "who rolls his R's in his North American way."[4] Neither of these figures plays any other role in her narratives, except to provide a negative image. Are they real people or merely

---

4. Arundhati Roy, *Power Politics* (Cambridge: South End Press, 2001), 36, 41.

invented? We never know, but Roy deploys these gratuitous fictions as objects of disdain, as if a marrowy physiognomy and a North American accent—rather than policy—were the true affront. Her writing will be discussed at greater length below in chapter 5 in relation to the anti-Americanism of the movement against globalization.

At this point, however, the concern is less Roy's more elaborate ideology than the fact that she is celebrated in the anti-American press and what this tells us about the ideology of anti-Americanism. For example, in the opening of her essay on "Mesopotamia," of April 2, 2003, in the *Manchester Guardian*, she conjures up the "adolescent American soldiers [who] scrawl colorful messages in childish handwritings" on missiles, and she dwells with a sort of lascivious interest on one private she saw in a CNN interview who "stuck his teenage tongue all the way down to the end of his chin." Her point is hardly sympathy with these "teenagers" who find themselves in a war—a plausible antiwar stance, concern for young people pulled into battlefield danger—but rather an explicit contempt for Americans, described as infantile, and their silly teenage behavior: this, she suggests, is the face of the enemy. What she subsequently musters as pseudoargument in the course of her diatribe is only secondary to the imagistic vilification of the opponent, classical propaganda, couched in a rhetoric tailored for a European audience: Americans are unmannered and have poor penmanship. The Indian author appeals to the elitism of European anti-Americanism that sees Americans as lacking culture.

Her focus on the motif of penmanship—irrelevant to policy substance but loaded as a cultural stereotype—is symptomatic of the role of anti-Americanism in the mainstream European press. A critique of Iraq policy is surely possible, but there is a surplus here that goes beyond the ostensible political substance.

It is apparently not the policy but the poor manners that matter. It is not the war that is the offense but the Americans themselves who are the real provocation to Roy's sensibility and to that of her readers. Opposition to the war in Iraq is ultimately therefore interchangeable with opposition to all the other aspects of American foreign policy. Opposition to the war does not lead to anti-Americanism; rather anti-Americanism, the primary affect, elicits opposition to the war. Iraq is really just one more item on a party platform. If pushed, the anti-Americans might concede that Saddam, the Taliban, and Milosevic were not particularly laudable (although we should not underestimate the degree of pro-Saddam sympathy, especially in France), but they only became issues because of that American foreign policy. Or to parse this even more closely: it is not what Americans do— since, in the end, most would be hard put to defend Milosevic, Saddam, and the rest—but the fact that it is Americans who act and not Europeans. It is therefore not European pacifism, a principled opposition to violence, that brings out the anti-American demonstrators but European passivity and an appeasement mentality that recoils at the American ability for action. The particular terrain where the action takes place becomes irrelevant. For the anti-American mind-set, the world—Iraq, Afghanistan, the Balkans—is always only a pretext, an emptied space, a blank sheet on which it tries to scrawl its own childish message: childish because incapable of political action.

What provokes the anti-American is American activism: not that America plays a particular role in the world but that it is in the world at all. Whatever the American action, the anti-American denounces it, particularly when the action is couched in a policy of defending the freedom to act, which in turn implies a set of democratic values. The absence of freedom in particular locales—Iraq, Afghanistan, the Balkans—is typically of concern

only for tiny nongovernmental organizations, not for mass protest movements, except when the United States intervenes.
There were never mass demonstrations in Paris, Berlin, or Bar-
celona against Milosevic, the Taliban, or Saddam. There were
never demonstrations for regime change. (The mass protest
movement only emerged when the authoritarian regime was
challenged by the forces of democracy). Before the war, Iraq was
noticed only because of the sanctions policy—an evil attributed
to the United States—and never because of the regime's character. In the context of the war, however, the anti-American
movement finds itself objectively, and often enough explicitly,
on the side of a dictator whom it had failed to criticize earlier;
and it is therefore even more scandalized by the American invo-
cation of democracy. The historical record shows that mass
demonstrations in Western Europe in the twentieth century
more often than not have involved direct or indirect support for
authoritarian leaders in order to oppose the United States.

This is an embarrassing political problem for the anti-American movement that pretends to be progressive but keeps wak-
ing up in bed with dictators. It shows willingness if not to
celebrate, at least to tolerate, authoritarian regimes, no matter
how brutal, in order to refrain from any association with capitalism, no matter how democratic. Any statism seems better than
freedom if freedom means a free market. This willingness to
rally around dictators and ignore the suffering in totalitarian
regimes is an extraordinary feature of the political culture of
Western Europe. Even after the demise of Communism, the
Communist taboos hold sway, as does its irreparably damaged
political culture. To be sure, anti-Americanism today is not primarily a matter of old-style Communism, but it is still stuck in
the political culture of the Communist age. Old habits die hard.
In fact, the moral hypocrisy of the anti-American movement

remains hopelessly trapped in the classic scenario of political blackmail that defined the limits of criticism in the century of totalitarianism. The traumatic scene of the Hitler-Stalin pact— the willingness of the Left to fall in line and oppose prospects for an antifascist war—continues to cast a long shadow on the possibility of political protest. It still promotes the sorry political formula: tolerance for an authoritarian peace, opposition to a democratic war. Hence the willingness to oppose regime change in Iraq: better to side, objectively, with Saddam Hussein than to support the American initiative for liberation. Peace at any price.

Brecht

This remarkable willingness to side with miserable regimes in order to avoid supporting the democracy of the United States repeats the pattern of the left in the years 1939 to 1941: the willingness to sacrifice substantive principles in the name of political expediency. It is useful therefore to turn back to that historical moment to see how one author in particular, the play-wright Bertolt Brecht—a Marxist, close to the Communist movement, and an exile from Hitler's Germany—viewed the political situation. Since he had every reason to fear the Nazi regime, the peace between the two totalitarian dictatorships could hold no appeal for him, despite his own Communist sympathies. Nonetheless, he had to overcome many predispositions, the political correctness of his day, before recognizing the possibility that the West—Western capitalist democracies and Great Britain in particular—was ultimately worth supporting as a potential opponent to Hitler.

For a brief moment, the Marxist Brecht caught a glimpse of how capitalist democracy represented a more plausible opponent to Nazi totalitarianism than did the Communism of Stalinist Russia. In two passages in his journals, he managed to work his way out of the politically correct Stalinist antiwar stance, the toleration for repressive peace, and came to advocate the democratic war. Despite his standard leftist starting points—anticapitalist, antibourgeois, antinationalist, and antiwar—he was ultimately able to comprehend how a willingness to wage war, to celebrate national identity, and to cultivate patriotism were desirable, at least in the context of patriotism within a democracy and a war against fascism. To do so, to recognize where the best hope lay for fighting Hitler, required a profound shift in his political instinct to reject war as such. He had to venture out of the ideological confines of Communism and its abstract idealism to embrace instead the vision of a heroic engagement in the drama of struggle. In order to fight for freedom, he had to escape from dogma. Brecht's successful, albeit brief, political opening provides a standard with which we can measure the ideological character of anti-Americanism.

In Scandinavian exile from Hitler's Germany, Brecht watched Europe collapse: "france fell at the maginot line, that underground 5-storey hotel, what an embodiment of parasitical french capital investment!" (journal entry of June 28, 1940).[5] After the French capitulation, would England fight? Brecht had his doubts, in the context of the Hitler-Stalin pact and the Communist opposition to war. In fact, Brecht had his own inclinations to oppose both militarism and nationalism. After all, he had begun his writing career as a schoolboy during the First World War with an attack on the Roman poet Horace's *dulce et decorum est pro patria mori*, the famous verse declaring that it is sweet and honorable to die for one's homeland, and he was him-

---

5. Bertolt Brecht, *Journals 1934–1955*, trans. Hugh Rorrison (New York: Routledge, 1996), 71.

self the author of the fiercely antiwar poem "Legend of the Dead Soldier." Having witnessed the devastation that the First World War caused to Germany, especially to his generation, Brecht was inclined to an antiwar position and, even in the changed circumstances of 1940, he was an unlikely candidate to endorse the mission of the English army. Yet despite his pacifist leanings and despite the Stalinist tilt against war and against the Western democracies through the pact with Hitler, Brecht began to explore the prospect for British participation in a possible democratic war, even before the fall of France. These explorations involve two key points where war and literature overlap.

Throughout Brecht's oeuvre, the Anglo-American world carries negative associations of capitalism and crime, from the London of *The Threepenny Opera* to the Chicago of *Arturo Ui*, and of course the elegiac poetry of the exile years in Hollywood. These same terms of disparagement continue in contemporary anti-Americanism, so Brecht's coming to grips with England can be taken as an alternative resolution of some of the same cultural problems: Brecht could come to embrace democratic England as a force against Hitler in a way that today's anti-Americans refuse to support the United States in the war against Saddam Hussein. Of course, Brecht, who cultivated a tough-guy image, felt some affinity with the masculine brutality that he associated with England, but this predisposition stood increasingly under the ideological censor of standard anti-militarism and Communist dogma. Trying to come to grips with England, however, he gradually overcame this resistance, at least partially.

In order to understand England, the writer Brecht, not surprisingly, read literature and history. In a remarkable journal entry of February 2, 1940, he reports on his reading Thomas Macaulay's essay on the early eighteenth-century poet Joseph Addison. It is here that Brecht encounters the liberal revolutionary England, in the wake of the Glorious Revolution of 1688, with its burgeoning public sphere in which literature took on a prominent role. As Macaulay put it, "Now the press was free, and had begun to exercise unprecedented influence on the public mind. Parliament met annually and sat long. The chief power in the State had passed to the House of Commons. At such a conjuncture, it was natural that literary and oratorical talents should rise in value."[6] It is hardly surprising that Brecht, the advocate of an engaged literature and a political theater, would find this cultural model appealing, in contrast to what Macaulay disparaged as the "servile literature of France,"[7] with its deep dependence on the power of the monarchy. Brecht concludes that English literature is strong "because a national life existed and the bourgeoisie came to power at an early stage"[8]—in contrast to German backwardness, without nationhood and without a national market. In other words, Brecht attributes the success of British literature to the vitality of nationhood and the energy of the market economy of the "bourgeoisie." Those are certainly not the typical values associated with communism, and the Marxist Brecht immediately glosses his own remark with an expression of surprise and despair: "what criteria!" At odds with his past, he finds himself compelled to reconcile his admiration for the English cultural achievement with an initial distaste for the precondition of that same cultural success: liberal capitalism. For it is precisely that market-based political economy that supported the culture that—Brecht reports—promoted technological progress and an empirical worldview and epistemology.

6. Thomas Babbington Macaulay, "The Life and Writings of Addison," in Macaulay, *Essays on Milton and Addison* (New York: Longmans, Green, and Co., 1900), 112.

7. Ibid., 115.

8. Brecht, *Journals 1934–1955*, 69.

German literature, he complains, is backward and idealistic, whereas British literature is up-to-date and engaged in the materiality of the real world.

Brecht then proceeds to draw these points from the critical debate on Addison's poem "Campaign," which celebrated the Duke of Marlborough's defeat of the French and Bavarian armies on August 13, 1704, at the Battle of Blenheim, a turning point in the War of Spanish Succession. The more literary his argument gets, the more pertinent it is for an analysis of political ideology. Thus, Brecht reports on how Dr. Johnson applauded Addison's use of concrete metaphors as exemplifying the advantage of the particular over the general: instead of bland generalizations or abstract connections, the comparisons are apt and grounded in reality. For Brecht, this concreteness of Addison's language and thought is tied to a model of heroic individualism: the hero who acts in the real world, instead of losing himself in cloudy vagueness. Addison's praise poem of Marlborough's military success is therefore simultaneously a celebration of the individualism of British liberty over the continental servitude of the absolutist French state. To cite Addison on Marlborough's army:

> . . . with native freedom brave
> The meanest Briton scorns the highest slave.[9]

For Brecht reading Macaulay reading Addison, the eighteenth-century battle of modern Britain against monarchist France represents a precedent for what Brecht hopes would ensue: a campaign by Britain—and the United States—pursuing

9. Joseph Addison, "The Campaign, A Poem to His Grace the Duke of Marlborough, 1705," *The Penn State Archive of Samuel Johnson's Lives of the Poets*, ed. Kathleen Nulton Kemmerer, http://www.hn.psu.edu/faculty/kkemmerer/poets/addison/campaign.htm.

the values of liberty and freedom against the oppressiveness of
the continent. German literature, in contrast, remains for Brecht
effetely idealistic and underdeveloped, fundamentally unable to
compete with the cultural revolution unleashed by the liberalizing dynamism of England.

Yet Brecht remains hesitant: the values of freedom and capitalism, nationhood and military strength are tough medicine for
him to swallow, burdened as he is with his Communist loyalties
and Central European pessimism. However, the February journal entry on Macaulay still preceded the fall of France. Once the
Germans were in Paris, suddenly the Nazi threat loomed much
larger, and by August we find him struggling again with his
own resistance and hesitations. He reports that he has
"skimmed"[10] Matthew Arnold's edition of Wordsworth—his
underlining the brevity of his reading betrays an embarrassment
to have to admit that he has been reading this presumably conservative literature—but he pushes immediately to the conclusion that it is dangerous "to lay down the law," which, in this
context, means to condemn this literature as "petty bourgeois":
the dogmatic judgment his Marxist aesthetic would most likely
have reserved for Wordsworth's poem "She Was a Phantom of
Delight." In other words, Brecht is announcing that the standard
Marxist ideological rejection is wrong.

As Robert Kaufman has shown, Brecht works out his own
aesthetic agenda here;[11] but he is also working out a politics, a
willingness to accept the progressive character of a democratic
capitalist culture personified by the British citizen-soldier in
wartime: "the individual petty bourgeois currently patrolling the

10. Brecht, *Journals 1934–1955*, 90.
11. Robert Kaufman, "Aura, Still," *October, no.* 99 (Winter 2002), 73–74,
note 46.

fields of england equipped with a shotgun and a molotov cock-
tail ('as used against tanks in the spanish civil war,' so a general
assured us on the wireless)."[12] Whom does the Marxist Brecht
celebrate here? It is not a mythic proletarian revolutionary or a
Communist cadre but the really existing citizen of a capitalist
bourgeois society, who, moreover, carries the emblem of the
antifascist fight, a weapon from the Spanish Civil War. But if
this democratic and capitalist society has, as Brecht insists, a
claim on a poetry that can "conjure up situations more worthy
of the human race," he has effectively retracted his youthful
attack on Horace: it is, so it turns out in the summer of 1940,
proper to fight for one's country, and poetry can provide sweet
comfort. Brecht has moved from support for the repressive
peace to approval of a war fought for democracy.

Brecht goes on to comment on the poem at hand, Wordsworth's "Phantom of Delight." He distances himself from
Wordsworth's suggestion that art serves only "to haunt, to star-
tle, and to waylay." While Wordsworth seems to suggest that a
poem is only about romantic beauty, Brecht calls for poetry to
do more. Nonetheless, his comments follow the movement of
the poem, which makes its way from a ghostly "apparition" or
"phantom" to the recognition of reality and then from reality to
an affiliation of art and freedom, or in Wordsworth's words:
"Her household motions, light and free, / And steps of virgin
liberty." Tracing the movement of the ideal apparition to the
material embodiment of lived life, Wordsworth's poem in fact
even goes beyond Brecht's own materialism, beating him at his
own game:—unless one reads Brecht's meditation on the
urgency of poetry for the soldier in the field as a commentary

12. Brecht, *Journals 1934–1955*, 91.

on the poem's telos. It was, one can conclude, a Wordsworthian "virgin liberty" that had fought in Catalonia, and so Brecht hopes, the same spirit of liberty will rally to defend England. Making freedom real is the beautiful: an aesthetic proposition where Brecht and Wordsworth, the Communist and the romantic, overlap.

Brecht's engagement with English literature has multiple components: autonomy, aesthetics, individualism, the mercantile ethos of capitalism, and the heroic ethos of war. Facing the danger posed by the authoritarian state on the continent, Brecht turned to the alternative: the parliamentary England of Addison's day that challenged Bourbon domination of the continent around 1700, and, a century later, Wordsworth's England of 1800 that defeated Napoleonic imperialism. Would the English-speaking world similarly withstand the Nazi threat of Hitler's *Festung Europa*, "fortress Europe"? Analyzing the British culture that could support the democratic wars—the poetry of Addison and Wordsworth—Brecht comes to admire it, even if he would never make it fully his own. Nonetheless, for the moment of 1940 at least, he could overcome his illiberal predispositions and express esteem for the democratic petty bourgeoisie, hoping that British capitalism would be able to live up to its historical legacy and act against fascism. His admiration for the soldier in the field, radiant with the aura of Wordsworth and the legitimacy of antifascism, is the diametrical opposite of Roy's disdain for the democratic soldier, with his childish scrawl and bad manners. The passages show Brecht working toward a rapprochement with the liberal institutions of England and the emancipatory character of bourgeois, which is to say, capitalist, life: for this same substance, shifted to the United States, today's anti-American only has contempt.

Anti-Americanism: A European Ideology

Is anti-Americanism an endogenous formation, the consequence of internal European cultural processes, or does it reflect
genuine differences between Europe and the United States? This
chapter began exploring the first model, according to which the
enemy is understood to be a retroactive construction, necessary
for the constitution of an identity. It followed that anti-Americanism had little to do with reality, or with real conflicts, and
much more to do with cultural traditions and stereotypes. Yet
Brecht's reflections of 1940 suggest an alternative account. At a
particular point in history, he was able to shift loyalties from
one culture to another, from continental ideologies of dogma to
British liberalism and liberty. For all his Central European illi-
beralism (which is shared by today's European anti-American
movements), he nonetheless imagined a personal rapprochement with the enemy, the culture across the channel. Brecht, the
son of Augsburg, accepted Marlborough's victory at Blenheim
and all that that implied—parliamentary ascendancy, commercial culture, military prowess as a progressive force, and, ultimately, autonomy aesthetics. This was no longer a one-sided
story but a clash of civilizations; on the one hand, a "servile
literature,"[13] associated with the authoritarian states of the continent, and on the other, a democratic civic life prepared to
defend itself. Brecht locates this militant democracy in English
culture; it is the same Anglo-American culture that is the target
of the anti-American mentality.

Yet these two explanations seem to be mutually incompatible: either anti-Americanism is the product of its own internal
ideological fantasies or it is the effect of real differences between

---

13. Macaulay, *Life and Writings of Addison*, 115.

Europe and the United States. The model of an animus driven by internal concerns and therefore characterized by the loss of external reality would presumably exclude the thesis of a real-world distinction between the cultures of the Atlantic and the continent, between commercial parliamentarianism on the one hand and regulatory regimes of state authority on the other. If there is indeed a conflict between these two orders—with social, cultural, and political implications—then it is less obvious that the animus is merely the expression of an independent instinct. So we face again the alternative between explanatory models for European anti-American hostility as either symmetrical or asymmetrical.

When anti-Americanism claims to be a response to specific American policies, it fits the dramatic model: policy conflict produces hostility. Yet, as we have seen, this self-presentation in fact typically invokes American policy only as a pretext. Too many features of anti-Americanism as a rhetorical and cultural phenomenon call this dramatic explanation into question. At best, it dwindles into a matter of lyric drama, just so much fantasy and fairy tale. In this sense, it is telling that European anti-Americanism succumbs repeatedly to its own tales of Arabian nights: the warning that American policy will ignite the "Arab street" with unforeseeable consequences. Yet this fiction has always proven itself a projection, a European desire staged as a fantasy against an Orientalist backdrop. The real issue of anti-Americanism is not the Arab street but the streets of Paris and Berlin and, in particular, their masquerading in exotic costumes as if they were the "Arab street." Far from toppling states in Jordan or Pakistan, the street demonstrations have only strengthened regimes in France and Germany; indeed the anti-American marches in Europe have in effect just been large progovernment rallies. The animosity toward the United States can be projected onto the rest of the world because for the anti-American the world has been emptied of meaning. The appeal to the Arab street involves no empathy with the Arab world; on the contrary, that street is only invoked in order to manipulate its image to carry out a European agenda, rather than to address an American policy.

This anti-Americanism has little to do with specific American policies. It is not about changing American action in the Arab world but about distinguishing Europe from the United States—that is, inventing a European identity as an alternative to the United States. This anti-Americanism is therefore indeed endogenous (a matter of European identity formation) and, ultimately, prepolitical (i.e., primarily cultural) as further shown by the inconsistencies in the local form it takes in different venues. If the point were a reasoned opposition to a specific policy, then one would expect the same argument to be made in different European countries. Instead, the mentality involves considerable local variation. In Germany, one finds the plethora of metaphors designed to exculpate the German past: Bush as Hitler, the bombing of Baghdad as the bombing of Dresden, the attack on the World Trade Center as the burning of the Reichstag. These displacements in fact tell us little about the United States, but they indicate a disturbed relationship to the troubled German past and a desire to resolve it through the expression of animosity. These metaphors make little sense elsewhere. In France, in contrast, a much more pronounced antisemitism contributes to the movement culture, including physical violence, in ways (for various reasons) less likely in other European countries. In addition, the French imperative to position itself against the United States has to do with its own history and its fantasies about a lost world-power standing (the same power, after all, that Marlborough defeated at Blenheim).

Yet none of this has much to do with American policies. The

real goal is a European identity. Beyond the fantasies or the caricatures, we should look at the various components of real anti-Americanism, its political categories, to understand how it plays a role in the invention of a unified Europe: anti-American-ism as a European fantasy exercise. However, at the same time, and beyond local national variations, this unified Europe, which is coming into shape precisely under the ideological umbrella of anti-Americanism, does represent a real-world alternative and is, objectively, in a fundamental and exogenous conflict with the United States. There is a drama, so to speak, a polar opposition, between the United States and Europe, but it is one that the anti-Americans barely comprehend. The anti-American mass move-ment that opposes the United States understands itself as a pro-gressive force in history and points an accusatory finger, therefore, to the pacts with the devil that the United States made in the cold war. (Its prepolitical moralism precludes its facing up to the difficult complexities of a lesser-of-two-evils choice.) However, the Soviet empire is gone now, the cold war is over; and the United States has shifted aggressively to a foreign policy of liberalization, a fundamental challenge to authoritarian regimes, and, in a deep historical sense, a return to the principles that underlay the rational freedom of Addison, whom Brecht could so appreciate. It is that liberalization that emergent Europe resists: no regime change, ever. Anti-Americanism is the ideology of maintaining the status quo while also providing a foil against which Europe can define itself.

Anti-Americanism has emerged as an ideology available to form a postnational European identity. In that sense, it is endog-enous: not a response to an outside threat but an aspect of Euro-pean political and cultural transformation. For the European Union to be credible, it has to carry some meaning and stand for more than a bureaucratic apparatus. Yet Europe has no ideal

content of its own; its failure to show leadership in the Balkans
in the early 1990s—1992 was to have been the "year of
Europe"—robbed it of the opportunity to define itself credibly
through the values of human rights and democracy. It therefore
has to define itself negatively, against outsiders, through the
deployment of caricatured opponents. Anti-Americanism fills
this ideological gap. In place of the nationalist anti-immigration
mood of the 1990s, anti-Americanism permits a generalized
European hostility toward the paradigmatic nation of immi-
grants. Europeans can therefore indulge in xenophobia without
nationalism.

For individual European nations, the price of entry into a
unified Europe is the gradual renunciation of national substance;
this is a painful process, even in Germany, the country most
eager to shed any remaining national legacy. This price includes
a suppression of intra-European enmities. The European past is
invoked as teaching that war must be avoided at all costs. Therefore: peace at any price, even repressive peace, and a prohibition
on regime change, which was the common denominator
between the governments and the European street. Anti-Americanism is the other side of the coin of appeasement. These are,
moreover, not opportunistic positions but the necessary consequence of suppressing European nationhoods. As the irreversi-
ble transfer of authority to the supranational organizations of
the European Union takes place, a deeply felt democracy deficit
ensues. It is the direct result of the priority of regime (not to be
changed) over nation (scheduled for elimination): more and
more of European life is regulated by powers beyond electoral
control or even public transparency. The political theorist Carl
Schmitt long ago identified the process by which the power of
democracies shifts increasingly into the undemocratic and
arcane realms of closed committees and bureaucratic decision

making.[14] Unified Europe is the prime example of this process. It has burgeoned into the generalized postnational and postde-mocratic regime of multilateralism: government less by election and more by regulation. The international form of the same principle is represented by the United Nations (regarded by Europeans, strangely, as carrying some moral authority); domesti-cally, it implies the bureaucratic social state and the regulated economy, impervious to reform.

Anti-Americanism, as the endogenous ideology formation necessary for European unification, does however ultimately confront an alternative—the United States—and enter into con-flict with it. Both explanatory models hold. The objective sub-stance of the conflict involves the opposition between multilateralism and unilateralism. Leaving aside the polemical points to be scored regarding Germany's unilateralism in pre-maturely opting out of an Iraq campaign (regardless of a poten-tial U.N. decision) and similarly bracketing the character of the French role in the U.N. and the French abuse of this organiza-tion, one can nonetheless recognize that the choice between unilateralism and multilateralism points far beyond the tech-nicalities of international relations. A difference between two fundamentally distinct cultural worldviews is at stake. Multila-teralism involves, by definition, an infringement of individual prerogative and implies the deferral of responsibility to a regime of committees, which—as the political theorist Hannah Arendt would have put it—is a responsibility of no one. It has a conse-quence in domestic policy as well as international relations: the overcoming of egoism. The association of the United States with unilateralism, in contrast, involves a different notion of lib-

14. Cf. Carl Schmitt, *The Crisis of Parliamentary Democracy*, trans. Ellen Ken-nedy (Cambridge: MIT Press, 1985).

erty, outside the state and outside the suprastate. The European vitriol directed at the United States allows Europeans to enter the European community. It is however simultaneously—and dramatically—the expression of hostility to independence, both individual and national, and on a deeper cultural level, the distorted expression of the pain of having had to surrender local purviews to a supranational bureaucracy. Forced to renounce their particular pasts and their national instincts, Europeans condemn as archaic American nationhood, looking at it all the same with wistful jealousy. The enmity directed at the United States externalizes the pain of loss and protests against the unfairness: why has history permitted Americans to maintain a national identity, while Europeans feel compelled to surrender theirs? Mass demonstrations—much more a European form than an American—are the appropriate ritual for this identity loss, in which grief over one's fate is transformed into rage against another's fortune.

A different and better Europe, one that lived up to the best of its past and pursued its aspirations, might tell a different story. After all, it was once liberty that led the people, even in Paris. Instead, today, anti-Americanism serves as a peculiar social psychology, based on the collectivistic identity formation that provides an antireformist ideology for European unification. European anti-Americanism is the primary cultural and ideological substance for the otherwise only bureaucratic process of European unification. This was quite clear in German Chancellor Gerhard Schroeder's election campaign: opposing American policy in Iraq was part of opposing *amerikanische Verhaeltnisse* (American conditions in general), meaning economic reform and deregulation. It remains to be seen whether Schroeder in Germany or the Chirac-Raffarin team in France will be able to cash in on their anti-American popularity in order to pass unpopular

economic reform. The more likely outcome is at best a minimally modified version of the status quo. The opposition to
regime change is, in the final analysis, about preventing any
change in the welfare-state regimes of Western Europe. Better
indolence than independence.

   Having probed the origins of European anti-Americanism
as part of the identity formation of unified Europe, we can recognize the alternative models of the post–cold war world,
which replace the myth of the Atlantic community of values.
During the missile debate of the 1980s, Cornelius Castoriadis
criticized the anti-NATO peace movement's willingness to subordinate all values to peace.[15] Not all qualities of life should be
sacrificed in order to maintain peace. The terrain is not much
different in the context of the war on terror. A European predisposition to accept the status quo and to do nothing rather than
to take risks, no matter how dire the situation, contrasts with an
American predisposition to assert independence and insist on a
responsibility to act, individually and as a nation. It is, however,
ultimately not the American actions themselves but the European inability to act that provokes anti-American rage.

---

15. Cornelius Castoriadis, *Devant la guerre* (Paris: Fayard, 1981).

4 ✷
Saddam as Hitler

Anti-Americanism has multiple dimensions. After examining the German data in chapter 1, in chapter 2 we explored several cultural and historical variants of anti-Americanism: first, an antimodern, predemocratic tradition; second, the legacy of communist ideology; and third, a contemporary, postdemocratic hostility to national sovereignty as such. Each version pushes anti-Americanism in a different direction. Chapter 3 looked at the tension between fantasy and reality in anti-Americanism, its ideological standing, and the role that anti-Americanism plays in the definition of an emerging identity for unified Europe. It is, however, obvious that current anti-Americanism has erupted in relation to the two Iraq wars. Although the various discourses of anti-Americanism refer to many issues, both political and cultural, it was clearly the confrontation between Washington and Baghdad that fueled the anger of the European street. Anti-Americans denounce the United States largely because it deposed Saddam Hussein.

The first Iraq war was fought to end the Iraqi occupation of Kuwait. The second Iraq war was fought to end the Iraqi regime. Both wars, however, were fought in terms of a metaphor: Saddam as Hitler. As this chapter will show, the terms of the metaphor shifted over time. At first the analogy had the narrow meaning of pointing out the unprovoked annexation of foreign territory: just as Hitler had invaded Czechoslovakia, Saddam had swallowed Kuwait, both transgressions against internationally recognized borders. Quickly, however, even during the first Iraq war, the metaphor came to signify the brutality of the Iraqi regime or, rather, the brutality of the Iraqi regime in its occupation of Kuwait. During the second Gulf war, the use of the metaphor became more emphatic: the brutality of the Iraqi regime to the Iraqi population itself and, especially, to ethnic minorities (e.g., the Kurds, the treatment of whom displayed a genocidal character). Moreover, the nature of the international threat posed by Iraq changed. Rather than being viewed as a local bully endangering its neighbors, Iraq came to be understood as the carrier of weapons of mass destruction, representing a much graver danger to countries much further away. On the one hand, the global threat associated with Iraq echoes the classical totalitarian aspiration to world domination; on the other, it is the function of a changed security perception after September 11.

The question of Iraq is central to the understanding of current anti-Americanism for two different reasons. As noted, the Iraq wars are the primary casus belli of the anti-Americans against the foreign policy of the United States. On a deeper level, however, the metaphor of Saddam as Hitler can lead us to a better understanding of what is at stake. For large parts of the American public, a war against totalitarianism remains just and worthwhile. For large parts of the public in Europe—the continent that incubated the two totalitarianisms that dominated the last century—a preference for appeasement prevails, and this difference turns into anti-Americanism.

However, the willingness to accommodate reprehensible

regimes is not only a European phenomenon, and clearly significant parts of the American public were opposed to the war. It is as if the judgment on totalitarianism had somehow softened since the collapse of Communism: not that one can find many defenders of the great dictators of the past but simply that the condemnation of Nazism and Communism no longer convincingly provides the orientation for the moral compass of many. So it is not surprising that George W. Bush's characterization of the Ba'ath regime as "evil" could be viewed as simplistic by a contemporary sensibility reluctant to distinguish between right and wrong, especially in Europe. It is not that anyone mounted much of a positive defense of Saddam Hussein's regime, but there was clearly reluctance to challenge it: Would it not be more comfortable just to ignore brutal regimes? Not everyone supported a war against Hitler, so it is not surprising to find an appeasement camp with regard to the metaphoric Hitler.

The Iraq wars posed the question of totalitarianism, both in terms of the metaphor of Saddam as Hitler and in terms of the real character of the regime, as will be discussed in this chapter. However, the wars also revealed the complex relationship of outsiders, so-called world opinion, to totalitarian regimes: though some witnesses can muster the resolve to confront evil, there is always a large appeasement camp with a strong desire to ignore, minimize, or even accommodate Hitler, Saddam, and their ilk. Therefore the historical question of totalitarianism is inextricably related to the contemporary question of moral judgment. Examining the metaphor of Saddam as Hitler allows us to reexamine the judgment on totalitarianism and thereby explore important inclinations in contemporary political culture. Germans born after 1945 sometimes asked their parents what they had done under the Nazi regime. Why had they failed to resist? History will eventually pose the same question to those who would have preferred to protect Saddam's regime from change.

The German Lesson

Weimar Germany has long stood as the prime example of a democracy that failed and turned into the cradle of totalitarianism. This teleology from Weimar to Hitler anticipated the many failed democracies of the twentieth century, and it stands as a cautionary note for current and future democratization prospects. Today we continue to ponder Weimar culture to understand the vulnerability of democracy and the potential for totalitarian outcomes. Nazi Germany casts multiple shadows on the mass-murderous landscape of the twentieth century, and Weimar remains pertinent as long as mass destruction haunts the modern world.

Yet the paradigmatic significance of the failure of Weimar and the establishment of Nazi Germany is frequently obscured or distorted by certain misconceptions, which deserve interrogation. First, it is an illusion to believe that there is an intellectually viable strategy to identify this Nazi modernity as distinctively belonging to a "right," and therefore different from a "left," modernity in a substantive way that is more than merely about the externals of party affiliation. There were left and right strands within National Socialism itself, and in any case what made the regime so central to the twentieth century was its totalitarian and genocidal character, which exploded the left-right mold.

Second, it is equally misguided to approach the Nazi regime primarily as a cultural (and especially as an aesthetic-cultural) phenomenon, associated with the establishment of something reasonably described as cultural hegemony. This cultural approach explicitly avoids politics as well as the degradation of politics into coercion and violence. Moreover the solely cultural approach to totalitarianism quickly runs into the temptations of cultural relativism, as if the Nazi worldview were just one possible choice among many, and therefore not subject to condemnation.

Finally, perhaps because of the growing distance from 1945, an underlying historicist tone has emerged that suggests that the Nazi era belongs to a completed past, a period in some once-upon-a-time epoch that has little to do with our contemporary condition. In this case, it would follow that the experience of that era has little pertinence to our thinking and institutions and that the totalitarian and mass-destructive potential played out in Germany in the 1930s and 1940s has no lessons for our contemporary predicament.

These three predispositions—accepting the conceptual viability and relevance of the left-right distinction, particularly regarding the emergence of the Nazi regime; the privileging of a cultural explanation and the attendant cultural relativism; and the historicizing distance indicating a diminished urgency to the question of totalitarianism—exemplify intellectual failings in the age of a relativist sensibility. To cut through some of these current misconceptions and recapture the standing of Hitler's Germany for political theory, it is productive to dwell on the current political metaphor, Saddam as Hitler, which can help us ferret out issues in the nexus of totalitarian regimes, political violence, and mass culture. Comparing Nazi Germany and Ba'athist Iraq, we can try to refocus the question of totalitarianism and its implication for political culture. In particular, this comparison can help clarify the three problems mentioned above and address certain lacunae in contemporary discussions of both regimes.

Regarding the left-right distinction: it makes little sense to claim that Nazi Germany was somehow of a "right" and that Stalinist Russia was then of a "left." Perhaps this distinction holds in the nuances of their respective discourses, but the overwhelming feature of totalitarianism, the destructive power of the unlimited state—the diametrical opposite of any ethos of limited government—outweighs those distinctions in style, and in any case, that destructiveness was not the function of being "right" or "left." As long as we pretend that National Socialism was of the right, then the parallel between the totalitarianisms of Hitler and Stalin is missed, and the history lesson of the twentieth century just becomes political bias. Saddam's Iraq is a case in point for the obsolescence of the political designations of left and right; to paraphrase a familiar slogan, it was neither left nor right but just terrible. It derived directly both from Hitler and Stalin in specific intellectual, political, and symbolic terms. Like both, it involved a regime in which the personality of the leader was central and stood in a dialectical relationship to a manipulative ideology of the mass: in the totalitarian world, the call for "mass cultures" implied the empowerment of great dictators.

The case of Iraq also calls into question cultural approaches to the Nazi regime, which naturally ascribe a central analytic standing to "Nazi culture." Was the contemporary credibility of the totalitarian regime genuinely a matter of a cultural consensus achieved through the successful dissemination of a plausible belief structure? Shall we really believe that the Nazi film and propaganda apparatus successfully convinced the German public that all was right with their world? No totalitarian regime has really been a cultural success in this sense. The alternative explanation, suggested by the case of Iraq, is the hypothesis of a "Republic of Fear," to use exile dissident writer Kanan Makiya's term: a regime in which violence, threats of violence, and enforced complicity in violence are overwhelming and form the basis for the stability of the state. This is not a cultural normalcy but a reign of terror. Following this line of thought with regard to Nazi Germany, one can inquire into the character of the totalitarian state as a regime of terror and angst, rather than as a merely distinctive cultural style.

Finally, if Saddam was like Hitler (and obviously the point is not the assertion of absolute identity but a challenge to consider similarities), then to what extent is the outside world's response to Saddam like the earlier response to Hitler? It is here that the discussion of Saddam as Hitler overlaps with the question of anti-Americanism. The point is not only to consider the intentional political allegory—we fought Hitler therefore we must fight Saddam—but to remember how great the reluctance to fight Hitler was. That historical appeasement mentality can help us understand the contemporary reluctance to confront Saddam. The international response to Hitler did not, after all, start in Normandy. There were long years of denial and deferral. Observers inside Germany and abroad minimized Hitler's importance in Weimar, and even after the Nazi accession to power in 1933, there was extensive acceptance, appeasement, and tolerance. Calls for "regime change" were not common.

Most egregious of course was the deep resistance in "world opinion" to believing the accounts of mass murder. A feature of modern world opinion is precisely this preference to avoid facing violence, as well as the fascination with authoritarian leaders (consider the popularity of dictators such as Stalin, Castro, and Mao in what are otherwise Western democracies). The metaphor of Saddam and Hitler is therefore also an opportunity to think through the psychology of this response to totalitarian leaders and the states they command. Why is it easier to talk about instruments of violence, the weapons of mass destruction, than to recognize victims of violence? For parts of the public, the presence of weapons of mass destruction was unquestionably more relevant than mass graves: a strange moral order, indeed.

Part of this dynamic has to do with the perverse consequence of a defining feature of enlightened modernity, tolerance, which is strangely taken to apply to criminal dictators too. Respect for the sovereignty of states—and their sovereigns—ranks well above any consideration of the well-being of citizens. Hence also cultural relativism, which quickly defends a reign of terror as just another way of life, for which we should show tolerance. The prewar political debate is a case in point, with the extensive resistance, even among otherwise human rights—oriented liberals, to discussions of regime change. This stance suggests the defense of sovereignty as such, no matter what the character of the regime, and therefore an inability to declare any regime unacceptable, which implies in turn the obligatory acceptance of any regime, no matter how bad. It follows that discussions of the domestic violence within another state are regarded with apprehension and mistrust, no matter how great the human suffering. Here the Saddam-as-Hitler metaphor takes another turn: the historical discounting of the reports of Nazi death camps represented the same mentality as the willingness to diminish the significance of Saddam's campaign against the Kurds. World opinion prefers to overlook genocide. Anti-Americanism results because the United States challenged this moral lethargy.

The Metaphor

In American political discourse, the metaphor of Saddam as Hitler dates from the period following the Iraqi invasion of Kuwait and referred at first solely to the phenomenon of international aggression. Thus George H. W. Bush said in his August 8, 1990, address announcing the deployment of U.S. forces to Saudi Arabia: "But if history teaches us anything, it is that we must resist aggression or it will destroy our freedoms. Appeasement does not work. As was the case in the 1930s, we see in Saddam Hussein an aggressive dictator threatening his neighbors."[1] In the same vein, one week later, on August 15, Bush spoke at the Department of Defense: "A half a century ago our nation and the world paid dearly for appeasing an aggressor who should and could have been stopped."[2] It was not difficult for the press to take the next step, name the dictator of the 1930s, and develop an analogy between Saddam and Hitler; but for official discourse the matter involved only the fact of aggression and its corollary, the historical lesson on the importance of refraining from policies of appeasement.

Two months later, however, the presidential account of his adversary changed significantly. In place of the fact of Iraqi aggression, the focus shifted to the Iraqi leader, now associated with negative attributes extending beyond the war of aggression. Perhaps this heightened rhetoric can be attributed to the more sensational imagery used by the press, with which the president or his speech writers had to compete; alternatively, the rhetorical shift may reflect the fall election campaign and the political need to amplify public interest through more pronounced statements. Surely part of the change, however, must be explained realistically by the continuing brutality of the Iraqi occupation and the only gradual recognition of this violence by

1. George H. W. Bush, "Address to the Nation Announcing the Deployment of United States Armed Forces to Saudi Arabia," August 8, 1990, http://bushlibrary.tamu.edu.

2. George H. W. Bush, "Remarks to Department of Defense Employees," August 15, 1990, http://bushlibrary.tamu.edu.

the outside world: it was no longer "just" a matter of the annexation of Kuwait by an occupying army but of a reign of terror
as well, which then compounded the significance of the Hitler
comparison. Thus in remarks at a fundraising luncheon for the
gubernatorial candidate Clayton Williams in Dallas on October
15, 1990, Bush asserted: "Hitler revisited. But remember, when
Hitler's war ended, there were the Nuremberg trials." The evil
of the adversary goes hand in hand with the expectation of a
conclusive act of justice.

To substantiate the need for a trial, however, Bush went into
detail at a Republican campaign rally in Manchester, New
Hampshire, on October 23, 1990:

> I am reading this great history of World War II. And I read the
> other night just about how Hitler, unchallenged—the U.S.
> locked in its isolation in those days, the late thirties—marched
> into Poland. Behind him—some of you will remember this—
> came the Death's Head regiments of the SS. Their role was to
> go in and disassemble the country. Just as it happened in the
> past, the other day in Kuwait, two young kids were passing out
> leaflets in opposition. They were taken, their families made to
> watch, and they were shot to death—15- and 16-year-old. . . .
> We're dealing with Hitler revisited, a totalitarianism and a bru-
> tality that is naked and unprecedented in modern times. And
> that must not stand."[3]

Although the Hitler metaphor was used in an effort to gal-
vanize public opinion, its development over a two-month
period highlights the complex range of distinct issues at stake:
aggression, appeasement, violence against civilians, totalitarianism, and, in particular, the personalization of the struggle with

---

3. George H. W. Bush, "Remarks at a Republican Campaign Rally in Manchester, New Hampshire," October 23, 1990, http://bushlibrary.tamu.edu.

an eye to war crimes trials. The latter point has to be seen not only as the rhetoric of the moment but as part of the tradition, perhaps distinctively American, of focusing on the personal responsibility of the adversary leader: Wilson's insistence on the Kaiser's culpability in the First World War, for example, as well as the criminalization of enemy leadership after the Second World War, both in Germany and in Japan.[4] More complexly and critically, one can suggest that the focus on the person of Saddam, this individualization of history, derives from multiple sources: an individualist ethos that looks for someone to blame as well as a mass-cultural propensity to simplify complex matters in terms of individual celebrities—that is, Saddam as Hitler, both as stars. Still, the focus on the individual, Saddam, was not only a rhetorical effect, driven by the dynamic of political discourse; it has to be seen primarily as a description of the priority of the singular personality, the political leader, in the totalitarian state.

Before turning to the implications of this personalization process, it is worth noting precisely what did not show up in the public discourse, in the press, or in presidential addresses regarding the similarities between Saddam and Hitler: multifold real historical ties between National Socialism and the Ba'athist regime in Iraq, which had turned into Saddam's personal rule. An Iraqi-inflected pan-Arabism began to develop soon after the end of the British mandate in 1932 and became the target of Nazi foreign policy, given Germany's strategic aspirations in Central Asia: the Nazi youth leader Baldur von Schirach visited

---

4. Cf. Daniel Moran, "Restraints on Violence and the Reconstruction of International Order after 1945," in *War and Terror*, ed. Frank Trommler and Michael Geyer, Vol. 14 (Washington: American Institute for Contemporary German Studies Humanities Series, forthcoming).

Baghdad in 1937, and the Futuwaa, a youth league modeled on the Hitlerjugend, was soon established. Nazi Germany (with Italy and, of course, the Soviet Union of the Hitler-Stalin Pact era) supported the al-Rashid coup of 1941, including the "Farhud," a pogrom against Baghdad's large Jewish population.[5] The coup was quickly suppressed, but it eventually became a mythic point of reference for the later-established Ba'ath Party, which celebrated the coup as "the first revolution for Arab liberation."[6]

We know that a key Ba'athist ideologue, Michel Aflaq, expressed admiration for Hitler, as did Saddam, and the Ba'a-thist pursuit of power has elicited comparisons to Germany; thus Nicholas Natteau wrote; "The street tactics of the Ba'ath against the ICP [Iraqi Communist Party] or suspected ICP sympathizers resembled those of Hitler's S.A. storm troopers during the street battles of the late 1920s in Weimar Germany."[7] This all suggests, however, that the Saddam-Hitler metaphor that emerged in response to the occupation of Kuwait in 1990 touched, if only accidentally, on a longer and more complex genealogical entwinement. The proximity of Saddam and Hitler implied by the metaphor is, therefore, not just an abstract comparison of distinct units but is grounded in the real history of Ba'ath ideology, Iraqi politics, and Saddam's personal admiration for Hit-

---

5. Majid Khadduri, *Independent: A Study in Iraqi Politics* (London: Oxford University Press, 1960), 172–73.

6. Kanan Makiya, *Republic of Fear* (Los Angeles: University of California Press, 1998), 151.

7. Nicholas Natteau, *Saddam over Iraq—How Much Longer? A Study of the Ba'thist Destruction of Iraqi Civil Society and the Prospects for Its Rebirth* (master's thesis, Boston University, 1997), www.joric.com/Saddam/Saddam.htm.

ler as well as Stalin.[8] It is not just a matter of comparing Saddam to Hitler for contemporary political reasons; there are also direct and multifaceted ideological connections.

The Leader

Where culture mobilizes the masses, they are probably following leaders. Totalitarian systems depend on the pairing of masses and leaders. Mass culture implies, in one variant or another, a cult of personality. Occasionally there are exceptions, when the utopias of free and leaderless masses circulate: for example, in the thought of Rosa Luxemburg, of the left-Communists whom Lenin famously denounced, or of some anarchists with their cult of spontaneity. But these utopian movements are typically contained and suppressed by more organizationally efficient institutions, and the masses are eventually subordinated to a party and a leader. Both in Germany and Iraq, the party overtook the people, and the leader came to eclipse the party.

The hypertrophic leader transforms the standing of the

8. "The lessons of 1963 had taught him that destroying civil society was not enough to ensure the IBP's [Iraqi Ba'th Party's] stay in power. Like Hitler, he now understood that this goal would require Ba'thizing not just the government, but the state, the military, and ultimately every nook and cranny of society. With this goal in mind, he was particularly attracted to the organizational methods used by Hitler to Nazify Germany. He understood that to ensure the party's complete domination over Iraq, society had to be regimented into the new Ba'thist order. According to one British journalist who visited Iraq in 1975, a government translator confided to him that Saddam Hussein's half-brother-in-law and head of intelligence, Barzan al-Tikriti, had asked him to procure books on Nazi Germany: 'He believed that Saddam himself was interested in this subject, not for any reason to do with racism or anti-semitism, . . . but as an example of the successful organization of an entire society by the state for the achievement of national goals.'" Efraim Karsh and Inari Rautsi, *Saddam Hussein: A Political Biography* (New York, Toronto: The Free Press, 1991), 89. Cited by Natteau, *Saddam over Iraq.*

"mass," a term that ceased to serve as a designation of the somehow really existing people and became instead a politically
charged category used to dominate and control. Thus Aflaq's
1979 celebration that "the role of the masses in the world has
come of age"[9] was not about authentic popular culture: it meant
instead that the Iraqi population had been redefined as a com-
pliant mass: the mass was represented by the party, and the party
was Saddam. In particular, Aflaq's assertion announced that the
political adversary, the Iraqi Communist Party, had been defin-
itively defeated and with it the category of class: the age of class
struggle gave way to the age of the Arab mass. Yet Aflaq's
announcement also pointed to the criminalization of any dissident or otherwise nonconformist individuality, incompatible
with the embracing and homogenizing category of mass. To be
individual would mean betraying the masses. This outcome is
consistent with the founding constitution of the Ba'ath party
and its assertion that "all existing differences between the members of the nation are superficial and false, and will be dissipated
within the anatomy of the Arab soul."[10] Individuality and difference were proscribed. Pan-Arabism, at least in the version Aflaq
bequeathed to Iraqi Ba'athism, was not only about a transnational solidarity, vaguely comparable to pan-Germanism (subtly
shifting politics away from citizenship in a nation-state to race,
a pseudobiological category at odds with the notions of citizenship) but also about the submission of the individual to the mass.
Pan-Arabism is ultimately one with the enforced collectivism
of Nazism as well as the left-modernist fascination with liqui-
dating individualism. Twentieth-century politicized mass culture, in its several inflections, on the Right and on the Left,

9. Makiya, *Republic of Fear*, 243.
10. Ibid., 197.

implies, tragically, a deep hostility to individual subjectivity and privacy. The echoes of this antisubjectivism reverberate through contemporary cultural theory (especially in the shadow of post-structuralism), which may explain the scholarly reluctance to address critically the illiberal regimes of totalitarian mass modernity.

The metaphor of Saddam and Hitler reappears however in a very different context, when Iraqi exile writer and dissident Kanan Makiya explores the character of Ba'athist politics by way of Hannah Arendt's study of totalitarianism, in particular with regard to the relationship of the masses to the leader in regimes of mendacity. Thus the Saddam-as-Hitler metaphor is not merely an artifact of George H. W. Bush's war rhetoric; it also serves the democratic Iraqi opposition in its efforts to make sense of the Ba'ath catastrophe. Makiya's interpretation of Iraq is refracted through Arendt's understanding of Nazi Germany. In both Nazi Germany and Saddam's Iraq, "truth" is whatever the leader says, no matter how absurd or implausible and, in fact, no matter how inconsistent or incompatible even with the leader's own earlier pronouncements. Thus Makiya, who is thinking about Iraq, cites Arendt, who is commenting on Hitler and Stalin: "The totalitarian mass leaders based their propaganda on the correct psychological assumption that . . . one could make people believe the most fantastic statements one day, and trust that if the next day they were given irrefutable proof of their falsehood, they would take refuge in cynicism; instead of deserting the leaders who had lied to them, they would protest that they had known all along that the statement was a lie and would admire the leaders for their superior tactical cleverness."[11]

11. Ibid., 115.

Makiya's point involves the character of the loyalty that the masses bring to the regime. It is not a matter of a consensus (i.e., the shared belief of a convinced public). It is not that the public somehow accepts the propagandistic disinformation as representing a substantive truth about which it might develop an informed opinion. Nor does the public succumb to an imaginably effective cultural-industrial manipulation or some restructured hegemony. All of these cultural-theoretical models fail. Instead, Makiya claims that Iraqis largely recognize the falsehoods as false, which instead of eliciting outrage leads to cynicism and even admiration for the ability of the leader to change positions. Indeed it is not even a matter of treating the statements of the regime as true—the expectation of a truthful government is simply not a given—but only as performance, and it is through performance, always more powerful than truth or rules, that Saddam acts out his predominance: ". . . the Leader's omnipotence is acted out dramatically, as though performed on a stage. Favors are bestowed on people in such a way as to break the very rules the Leader's state enforces . . . ; his freedom to act, even to break his own rules, is intentionally pitted against everyone else's profound unfreedom. The effect, however, is not to highlight the latter, but to confound it with the former."[12] In a context of universal falsehood, Iraqi society does not find sustenance in a successfully convincing propaganda apparatus, some "mass culture" that elicits support and authentic trust, but rather in the image of the great leader. Hero worship—that is, the worship of one hero—is central to the regime, which authorizes no room for disagreement or dissent. In other words, at stake is not an ideology of heroism that might be taken to call on all individuals to excel and to act heroically

12. Ibid., 116.

but rather a constant entwinement of the abjection of each individual, facing constant admonitions to abjure all particularity, and the focus on the one leader who is the collectivized nation. Saddam was Iraq in the sense of the Nazi slogan *Deutschland ist Hitler.*

It is worth observing Makiya follow Arendt in one further step, as he highlights the freedom that was absent in Saddam's Iraq. Freedom—in the Ba'athist tradition—is only the freedom of the nation as a whole, (i.e., a sort of decolonization as collectivism, and this is then transferred onto the political leader). There is no claim of individual freedom. Yet, Makiya poignantly develops an alternative position: "The notion of freedom as a political condition that only exists because of the capacity of human beings to be different, to be in a minority, and not have to think the same deathly 'free' thoughts." This version of freedom, he continues, "is absent in Iraqi society. When it arose in the modern era, it was snuffed out, first by the growing ideological hegemony of pan-Arabism and later by the social organization of the second Ba'athist regime [i.e., post-1968]. The absence not only of freedom but also of the very *idea* of this kind of freedom makes Saddam Husain's role-playing so effective."[13]

Makiya's claim regarding the political freedom in the human condition translates Arendt's political theory into Iraq. The definition of freedom in terms of a human condition obviously stands at odds with current academic dogma regarding essentialism and humanism; eventually the political implications of this intellectual baggage may become clear. In the context of this chapter, however, and the examination of the cross-national metaphor, what resonates is the suggestion of an underdevel-

13. Ibid., 116. Makiya consistently spells the name of the Iraqi dictator in this manner.

oped liberal tradition—a standard piece of thinking about historical German political culture—but also a nostalgia for a lost
opportunity. Makiya suggests that between the establishment of
a parliamentary monarchy in 1932 and the seizure of power by
the Ba'ath Party in 1968, liberalizing possibilities in Iraq did in
fact exist. The Ba'ath, who suppressed that tradition of freedom,
look back at the earlier era with disdain, celebrating only the
Nazi-supported 1941 coup. This historical vision of the dicta-
torial party is analogous to the Nazi memory of the Wilhelmine
era and the Weimar "system," both vilified as too liberal and too
free.

The Leader as Artist

Makiya's underscoring of Saddam's performance—his
drama and his role-playing—points to the prominence of the
leader as individual and as artist within the totalitarian system.
Similarly, the German author Thomas Mann once drew attention to aspects of Hitler's performance and its proximity to
aspects of the artist.[14] Saddam and Hitler as artists? One might
compare Hitler's early interest in painting with Saddam's
strange obsession with architecture.[15] Yet the point here is not
the artistic production as such but rather the performance of the
political leader as itself the act of art. The great leader of the
masses stages himself as an artistic genius, precisely as part of
his political presence. Facing the degraded masses, the leader
stands out and above them as a unique individual, the creative
genius: the artist. Saddam and Hitler both projected themselves

---

14. Thomas Mann, "Bruder Hitler" (1938), in *Essays*, Vol. 4, *Achtung, Europa!
1933–1938* (Frankfurt am Main: S. Fischer, 1995), 305–12.

15. Cf. Said K. Aburish, *Saddam Hussein: The Politics of Revenge* (London:
Bloomsbury, 2000), 265–66.

to the public as absolute and overriding, as two examples can amply demonstrate.

While Hitler denigrates the conformist masses, whom he regards as susceptible to propaganda, he heroizes great individuals, to whom he attributes the artistic qualities of freedom and creativity. Everyone else conforms and obeys, but the totalitarian leader as artist can break all the rules (as in Makiya's description of Saddam) while he asserts his particular individuality against the world. Thus Hitler writes in Ralph Manheim's translation of *Mein Kampf*: "Personality cannot be replaced; especially when it embodies not the mechanical but the cultural and creative element. No more than a famous master can be replaced and another take over the completion of the half-finished painting he has left behind can the great poet and thinker, the great statesman and the great soldier, be replaced. For their activity lies always in the province of art. It is not mechanically trained, but inborn by God's grace."[16] Different legacies compete within those lines: the opposition of the mechanical and the cultural, the cult of great masters, the priority of the aesthetic—all of these might be taken as aspects of the shattered cultural tradition of the educated middle class, the *Bildungsbürgertum*. Yet it is Hitler's insistence on irreplaceability, a resistance to exchange, that links his discourse to aspects of the aesthetic tradition: like the work of art and the artist, the politician too is absolutely original and fully unique. Where this claim becomes distinctively Hitler's, however, and where it stands absolutely at odds with Makiya's Arendtian appeal to difference in the human condition, is that—for Hitler—this uniqueness is the province of only a few, the great, the masters.

16. Adolf Hitler, *Mein Kampf*, trans. Ralph Manheim (London: Hutchinson, 1969), 320.

The paragraphs that follow plunge, characteristically, into Hitler's antisemitism. The virtue of irreplaceability does not apply to everyone. Yet Hitler does not exclude Jews alone. On the contrary, he claims that most of humanity is barred from the realm of the unique. Being genuinely individual is not part of the general human condition. Uniqueness is, on the contrary, the exclusive privilege of the few. Meanwhile, the many, the perpetually replaceable masses, depend on a few leaders, who are alone distinct. Thus Hitler continues: "The greatest revolutionary changes and achievements of this earth, its greatest cultural accomplishments, the immortal deeds in the field of statesmanship, etc., are forever inseparably bound up with a name and are represented by it. To renounce doing homage to a great spirit means the loss of an immense strength which emanates from the names of all great men and women."[17] Hence a vision in which the few great creators tower over the conformist mass and demonstrate their greatness through a distinctiveness that is—regardless of explicit field of activity—fundamentally artistic.

This priority of leadership in the context of mass society explains a characteristic aspect of *Mein Kampf,* the strange interspersion of autobiography in the political program. Individual personality—Hitler's memoir writing—pervades the political polemic throughout the book. Indeed this is the program announced in the preface to *Mein Kampf,* where Hitler states that the volume is intended not only to describe "the aims of our movement" and its development but also "to give an account of my own development."[18] There is, however, a strange ambivalence about the project. Hitler concludes the preface, to be sure,

17. Ibid.
18. Ibid., xlv.

with a monumentalizing gesture: "for a doctrine to be dissemi-
nated uniformly and coherently, its basic elements must be set
down for all time. To this end I wish to contribute these two
volumes as foundation stones in our common edifice." Writing,
he suggests, may guarantee eternal permanence and preclude
interpretive variance, despite the dissemination of the message.
Hence, the reassuring conclusion of the preface: he is putting his
message in stone to guarantee its immutability. Yet this follows
immediately on the unintentional expression of an underlying
doubt about the book: "I know that men are won over less by
the written than by the spoken word, that every great movement
on this earth owes its growth to great orators and not to great
writers." Hitler the orator seems to doubt Hitler the writer. Or
is it the pervasive suspicion of writing, literature, and the press
that leads Hitler to this paean to orality? The heavy edifice he
constructs in *Mein Kampf* recalls the Landsberg prison in which
he wrote the book, but the closing of the preface also takes on
an epitaphic character: a conclusiveness, an end, which would
only be mitigated by live oration.

The preface to *Mein Kampf* sheds light on the cultural character of totalitarianism with its tension between between writing
and oration and between permanence and vitality. This conflict
is symptomatic of the totalitarian condition: the leader is at the
center of the movement, but the cumbersome apparatus of the
movement (the party and its bureaucracy) may come to be at
odds with the principle of leadership, which requires the possibility of constant redefinition. The need to write, in order to
build an edifice, conflicts with the need never to be held to one's
word since truth is only contingent, whereas writing is permanent. Orality provides a flexibility that literacy, with its inher-
ently critical potential, undermines through its durability. As
creative artist, the leader can always say something new, with

little concern for consistency. It is this absolute elevation of the leader that is symptomatic.

Saddam Hussein imitated this elevation of the totalitarian leader that had been prefigured by Hitler and Stalin. In *Mein Kampf*, Hitler's autobiography intrudes into the political agenda. The Iraqi corollary, with a similar magnification of the leader, is the infamous Victory Arch in Baghdad. It is a grotesque monument, completed in August 1988 to celebrate the (dubious) victory over Iran, and unveiled in the midst of the genocidal *anfal* campaign against the Kurds. Saddam designed the monument himself, intending it as an Iraqi competitor to the Parisian Arc de Triomphe, but Saddam is present in the monument in a way that goes far beyond his having envisioned it. Just as Hitler, the individual, protrudes into the Nazi program of *Mein Kampf*, so too does Saddam, the person, dominate the Iraqi national monument.

Makiya describes the monument as follows: Two steel forearms "come bursting out of the ground like bronze tree trunks and rise holding a sixty-six-foot-long sword in each fist. The two swords cross to form the apex of the arch at a point roughly 130 feet above the ground. Each forearm and fist, with the steel frame on which it is fixed, weighs 40 tons. Each sword, made of stainless steel, weighs 24 tons. This steel . . . was made by melting down the actual weapons of Iraqi 'martyrs.' War debris in the shape of 5,000 real Iranian helmets, taken from the battlefield, are gathered up in two nets (2,500 helmets per net). . . . To look at the helmets in the knowledge that their scratches, dents, and bullet holes are real, that human heads might well have exploded inside them, is . . . breathtaking."[19] Indeed, it is

---

19. Kanan Makiya, *Cruelty and Silence: War, Tyranny, Uprising, and the Arab World* (New York: Norton, 1994), 209.

almost as breathtaking as the one defining characteristic of the monument, the bizarre fact that the two forearms are not sculpted objects but castings taken from plaster casts of Saddam's own arms and then enlarged. In 1991, still compelled to write under the pseudonym Samir al-Khalil, Makiya pondered this point: why a casting, which preserves all the imperfections, the scars, the veins, and the hair follicles of the forearms, rather than a sculpture that might have idealized the body parts? His answer: "Only casting renders absolute authority (which is singular and abstract, yet experienced in all the minutiae of daily life in Iraq) visible and corporeal, while retaining the aura of absolute uniqueness, so essential to the work of art even in this age of mechanical reproduction."[20]

The projection of the leader's irreducible uniqueness into the artistic edifice, in homology to *Mein Kampf*, displays the absolute priority of personal power. It is not some idea or the spirit of the nation that pervades this war memorial. It is the unquestionable authority of the lord and master, the totalitarian leader. The masses are instrumentalized, literally—they are made identical with their instruments of violence—in the swords made from the weapons of the Iraqi soldiers, or they are degraded in the display of the Iranian helmets (degraded and desecrated: elsewhere Makiya reports how the corpses of the victims executed by Saddam's police were denied ritual cleaning, thus preventing their entry into paradise). The infinite narcissism of the leader means that nothing else counts, reality dwindles away, and the world can be annihilated. As different as these two entities are, *Mein Kampf* and the Victory Arch, both demonstrate the same imperious standing of the leader. In terms

20. Samir al-Khalil (Kanan Makiya), *The Monument: Art, Vulgarity, and Responsibility in Iraq* (Berkeley: University of California Press, 1991), 6.

of political self-presentation, the metaphor—Saddam as Hitler—surely holds.

Culture and Violence

Saddam and Hitler: it is not difficult to ascribe to each a cultural penumbra, the writers, artists, and intellectuals who, sometimes bought, sometimes in voluntary delusion, pursued an affiliation with the totalitarian regime: Riefenstahl, Speer, Heidegger, Nolde, or the various Arab writers and Western architects who have benefited from Baghdad's largesse.[21] In this context, one can cite as well the cultural programs of the regimes, the celebration of particular traditions or the symbol-laden construction projects: Saddam chose to rebuild Babylon. He would often stage himself as the heir to ancient civilizations, receiving the law from Hammurabi, using bricks, on each of which his name was imprinted: the intrusion of the leader into monumentality, as much an act of possession and naming as Hitler's placing himself in the center of *Mein Kampf.*[22]

Did this sort of culture really matter? It remains an open question whether this cultural frenzy—writers' congresses, architectural competitions, museum exhibitions—played any significant role in generating support for the regime, as measured against the primary feature of life in the totalitarian state: fear of violence, including the moral degradation associated with complicity in violence. The contempt that the German author Ernst Jünger, referring to battlefield experience in the

21. *Cruelty and Silence* provides extensive discussion of how the Iraqi regime bought off Arab intellectuals to silence criticism and gain a public relations advantage.

22. Cf. Neil MacFaquhar, "Hussein's Babylon: A Beloved Atrocity," *New York Times*, August 19, 2003, A10.

First World War, could feel toward the aestheticizing world of bourgeois security can shed light on the tendency to treat the totalitarian regime as an aesthetic style. In Jünger's words: "Our blood is full of passions and feelings, that have no place at tea-time."[23] Or more explicitly anticultural: "This is not the time to read *Werther* with a tearful eye."[24] The existential reality of the battle stands at odds with the sentimentalism that Jünger associates with Goethe's novel *The Sorrows of Werther*. War, so Jünger implies, has no space for culture.

It is a time of violence, not of art. This implies, however, that the culture of the totalitarian regime—if "culture" is the right word at all—is not primarily its aesthetic works but the ubiquity of violence and fear. In this view, the Nazi regime was defined less by its various propagandistic art exhibits than by its brutality and murder, public and private. This is surely true of Iraq. Despite the elaboration of a Ba'athist ideology, with influences from Sorel (through Aflaq) and Fichte (through Husri),[25] it is not the credibility of that confused amalgam of intellectual history that held Saddam's Iraq together but rather fear. Khidir Hamza, a key defector from the Iraqi nuclear program, writes of viewing a film of a "party denunciation meeting" in which the members of the party elite were forced to shoot each other.[26] Makiya similarly describes the double strategy of public and private violence: the public hanging of Jews accused of espionage in January 1969, at the outset of the regime, attended by thousands; and the private torture, that concluded with sealed

23. Ernst Jünger, "Der Kampf als inneres Erlebnis," in *Sämtliche Werke Essays I: Betrachtungen zur Zeit* 7.1 (Stuttgart: Klett Verlag, 1980), 95.

24. Ibid., 39.

25. Cf. Makiya, *Republic of Fear*, 152.

26. Khidir Hamza, *Saddam's Bombmaker: The Terrifying Story of the Iraqi Nuclear and Biological Weapons Agenda* (New York: Scribner, 2000), 112–15.

coffins to keep the bodies invisible. "Fear is the cement that holds together this strange body politic in Iraq," writes Makiya: not ideology, loyalty, or even tradition. "The public is atomized and broken up, which is why it can be made to believe anything." Mass society in the totalitarian world is, in effect, not a mass at all, but the ruins of the former civil society and communities. Makiya continues: "A society that used to revel in politics is not only subdued and silent, but profoundly transformed. Fear is the agency of that transformation; the kind of fear that comes not only from what the neighbors might say, but that makes people careful of what they say in front of their children. This fear has become a part of the psychological constitution of citizenship."[27]

It is a terroristic society, and the description holds as much for Saddam's Iraq as it did for Hitler's Germany: cultures of fear, rather than art. Terror and the shame of complicity define individual lives. For example, for those Germans who viewed the boycott of Jewish stores in April 1933, enforced by Nazi paramilitary gangs, fear of facing similar threats and the shame of having stood by passively surely must have left traces that determined their subsequent relationship to the regime: a relationship of degradation and humiliation rather than of voluntary participation or ideological consensus. More important than the mobilized culture portrayed in Leni Riefenstahl's films, the Nazi reign of terror was defined by an immobilized conscience.

It is here that the German author Hans Magnus Enzensberger's February 1991 reflection on Saddam and Hitler ("Hitler's Successor: Saddam Hussein in the Context of German History") becomes pertinent. Enzensberger argues that in contrast to the standard dictators of the twentieth century, who were eager to

27. Makiya, *Republic of Fear*, 275.

enrich themselves and therefore calculable, Hitler and Saddam represent something different, a desire for destruction as such. Plausible goals or a serious ideology are absent. Rather than personal gain or principled ideals, their ultimate goal is annihilation, a deep death wish, from which their own people, indeed the leader himself, is not excepted. In Iraq and Germany, this annihilationist leadership could succeed because of the widespread feelings of national humiliation—the defeat in the First World War, the legacy of colonialism—and these instincts were then available for manipulation by the unlimited will to death of the totalitarian political leader. Thus Enzensberger concludes: "The enemy of humanity can arm himself with the combined death energy of the masses, which gives him power bordering on genius: the infallible sense for unconscious stirrings in his followers. He does not operate with arguments but with emotions that unhinge any form of logic."[28]

Enzensberger's account is at odds with Makiya's, particularly with regard to the description of the population: in Makiya's "republic of fear," the bulk of the population is terrorized and terrified. In contrast, Enzensberger sketches a fanatic and fanatically loyal population. The distinction is significant, but in both models the center of social life is destruction: the threat of destruction directed by the state toward the population—as well as toward external enemies—or the self-destructive vengeance attributed to the population in pursuit of a death that it desires. The experience in postwar Iraq confirms both visions. There is evidence that the bulk of Iraqis appreciate the end of Saddam's reign of terror, but there is also a hard core of

---

28. Hans Magnus Enzensberger, "Hitler's Successor: Saddam Hussein in the Context of German History," *Telos* 86 (Winter 1990–91), 156.

"dead-enders," blindly loyal to the leader and indifferent to the prospect of continued hardship for the Iraqi people.

Was there a totalitarian "culture" that was more than the fear that terrorized and atomized individuals felt? Enzensberger at least suggests that there was a kind of mobilized culture in the totalitarian state, but it was a mobilization directed not toward an imaginable victory but only toward devastation. Nazi architecture, understood in this sense, should not be thought of as best exemplified by the massive megalomania of Albert Speer's building plans but by the real-world leveling of European cities, the genuine goal of the Nazi imagination. In fact the same implies for the Allied destruction of German cities, an architecture of ruins, which, in Enzensberger's account, was somehow not the result of the Nazi military failings but the very goal of the Nazis from the start. The Nazis pursued total war as they sang, "until everything falls to pieces." Their goal was to transform the *Volk ohne Raum*—"people without space," the title of a pro-Nazi novel advocating German colonialism—into pure *Raum ohne Volk*, space without people, where human life has come to an end. It was American and English bombs that leveled German cities, but that destruction was the result of a death wish deeply embedded in the Nazi imagination from the start. Saddam's murders never numbered as high as the mass murder under Hitler or Stalin, but a similar process pertained: the program for mass destruction was directed against his own people as much as against external enemies.

Blissful Ignorance and Anti-Americanism

If the metaphor holds and Saddam is like Hitler, then how the world responded to Nazi Germany sheds light on how it has responded to Iraq. Of course, the analogy is not perfect, and the historical circumstances were different, nonetheless there is one striking similarity. In neither case did the egregious violence of the totalitarian regime lead directly to unanimous protests and opposition. On the contrary, in both cases the serious military engagement—the war against Nazi Germany and the war against Saddam's Iraq—took place only after extensive equivocation and denial. A desire to ignore violence prevailed, and that inclination grew stronger, the more terrible the violence. As far as Iraq is concerned, the question of compliance with U.N. disarmament mandates was long given pride of place and was split—in the interest of respecting state sovereignty, no matter how miserable the character of the state—from questions of the treatment of the domestic population, about which a grotesque and chilling silence prevailed. Even after the war, the mass graves simply count less than a determination about the weapons of mass destruction. We would rather not hear. The secret of domestic violence, in Iraq or elsewhere, is not easily addressed; indeed it is preferably ignored.

While the initial German lesson cited by George H. W. Bush in 1990 was the admonition against appeasing an international aggressor, there is surely another lesson as well: the urgency to refuse to accept the world's predisposition to remain impervious to genocide and terror. What is the iron law that makes world opinion—the editorial pages of leading newspapers, the U.N. committees, and the experts of the public sphere—so predisposed to ignore the news of violence, and are we condemned to obey this law? Surely the victims of violence want their story to be heard. For example, Makiya concludes an interview with Taimour, a young Kurd who, as a twelve-year-old, witnessed the mass destruction of his village and the killing of his family:

"If you could choose, what would you want to do in your
life now?

I don't know for myself.

Is there something you want out of life very much?"

Yes.

What?

To be a known person.

A known person?

Yes.

Known for what?

The *Anfal.*

Do you want to be known more for the *Anfal* or for being
a *peshmerga?*

For *Anfal.*

What do you mean 'known for *Anfal'?*

I want the world to know what happened to me."[29]

The problem is, however, that much of the world does not
want to know. The desire to be untroubled by other's suffering
is often greater than the sense of human compassion. The similarity of Nazi Germany and Saddam's Iraq is confirmed by the
comparable avoidance strategies that outsiders employed in
order to ignore. The severe violence of the totalitarian regime
elicits nothing more readily than silence among the well-meaning carriers of world opinion: mass murder often provokes less
protest than a trivial scandal in a run-of-the-mill city hall. As
Enzensberger put it, "Then, as now, the world did not want to
come to terms with what it confronted. Foreign governments
regarded Hitler as a statesman representing 'legitimate concerns,' whom one had to accommodate, with whom one had to
negotiate. The winners of WWI welcomed him as an 'agent of
stability,' as a trading partner, as a counterweight to the Soviet

29. Makiya, *Cruelty and Silence,* 199.

threat; in other words, one dealt with him on a normal political level and trusted that it was a matter of solving conflicts of interest."[30]

The flight into normalcy was not merely a matter of self-interest but also, indeed above all, a denial of the horror, a refusal to hear the news of the death camps, just as today Saddam's genocide is not given serious consideration, especially by opponents of the war. This is as true in the Arab world as in the democratic West: the man responsible for killing the most Muslims in history does not face much retrospective criticism among Arab leaders. Thus Mohamad Jasem al-Sager, the head of the Foreign Affairs Committee in the Kuwaiti People's Council, commented bitterly on Arab parliamentarians' silence regarding the evidence of mass killings under Saddam: "Is it possible that the representatives of the Arab nations refuse to abide by even the most basic duties of their profession—representing their people? Is it possible that they fail to utter a single word of sympathy for the thousands of victims of the Arab dictator? . . . Arab parliamentarians limit their condemnation to the Zionists and the foreign invasion and have purposefully forgotten the crimes committed under our noses. Would these Arab parliamentarians dare to hold the gaze of an Iraqi woman sitting at the grave of her murdered children? We have seen thousands of people gathering the remains of their relatives in plastic bags."[31]

Perhaps Arab parliamentarians have ideological grounds to avoid criticizing another Arab leader: a misguided ideology to be sure. Yet there was hardly a comparable rationale in the West for politicians and demonstrators to come to the defense of the

30. Enzensberger, "Hitler's Successor," 157.
31. MEMRI, *Special Dispatch Series*, no. 533, July 2, 2003, http://memri.org/bin/articles.cgi?Page=archives&Area=sd&ID=SP53303.

Iraqi regime—except the cowardly rationale of avoiding addressing the violence. In the end, it was left to the United States to respond to the fact of Saddam's genocide. George W. Bush called it "evil" and scandalized those segments of the cultural-relativist public who would have preferred to ignore it. Anti-Americanism derives from many sources, as we have seen in the previous chapters, but among these sources one figures quite large: the high moral standard that the United States has set, in the Iraq war and in fact since the Nuremberg Trials, with regard to Nazi Germany. Whether the United States has always lived up to these principles is another matter, but historical failings never disprove the validity of ideals. The United States has played an indispensable role in the wars against totalitarian violence and has thereby raised moral standards in world affairs. The United States has disrupted the blissful ignorance of a world opinion prepared to ignore suffering. Resentment results. Anti-Americanism is the expression of a desire to avoid the moral order and to withhold compassion from the victims of violence.

5 ✖

Anti-Americanism and the Movement against Globalization

Earlier chapters have traced the cultural and ideological character of anti-Americanism: how it acts like an obsession or prejudice, impervious to facts, and how it derives from deep-seated European anxieties about the "new world" and the promise it bears for democracy and capitalism. In addition, chapter 4 has shown how anti-Americanism burgeoned in the context of the Iraq war, the experience of which was colored by the memories of twentieth-century totalitarianism. In this chapter, we turn to a different inflection of anti-Americanism. Anti-Americanism is certainly not the same as the movement against globalization; indeed there are American opponents of globalization—as free trade—who are hardly anti-American in their cultural and political views. Nonetheless, there is a large overlap between antiglobalization and anti-Americanism, which this chapter explores.

In standard usage, the term "globalization" refers to the economic process of increased international trade and investment associated with a long-term decline in the cost of transportation and communication. The accelerated mobility of both capital and labor ensues, generating the flow of goods, services, and people across national-political boundaries. This international character of economic activity is hardly new; there is a long prehistory to international trade and long-distance migration. The spread of economic relations across the borders of states has been under way for centuries.

However, objective measurements are just one side of the story; subjective experience is another. Whether one sees globalization as a long-term feature of economic life or as a largely recent phenomenon, it is clear that the public discussion of globalization and, more precisely, the protest movement against globalization emerged suddenly during the 1990s, and this antiglobalization movement continues to resonate in many quarters around the world. (There is some irony in the fact that antiglobalization spread rapidly and with ease across international borders, exemplifying a certain cultural globalization: there is nothing more globalized than the opposition to globalization.) Given the articulation of antiglobalization sentiment in diverse contexts, it is not surprising that political motivations and sentiments are not uniform or homogenous. Hostility to globalization is driven by distinct interests and arguments in different locations: opposing McDonald's franchises in France is not necessarily cut from the same cloth as opposing free trade in developing countries. Nonetheless, there is a shared idiom of protest against globalization that characterizes a subculture from Berlin to Berkeley. At its center is an economic claim. Although most professional economists see free trade and anti-protectionism as preconditions for the production of wealth and overcoming poverty, the critics of globalization typically reject this neoliberalism and call in various, if often vague, ways for regimes of increased protectionism and regulation. On one level, the critique of globalization is therefore about the appeal for increased political intervention in economic processes.

Indeed, the critique of globalization has become the predominant form of anticapitalism in the post-Communist era. Antiglobalization is not only about a protest against transnational processes; it is also about a positive advocacy for expanded political restrictions on the economy. The collapse of the Soviet Union and its satellite states marked the conclusion of a history of an economic idea, the ideal of the planned economy associated with Communism since 1917; the remaining power of Communist parties in China, North Korea, Vietnam, and Cuba clearly has nothing more than a residual character. Communism certainly no longer projects a world-revolutionary project, as was once the case in the heyday of Russian prominence. Yet while the Communist critique of capitalism has essentially ceased to command any serious attention, the critiques of globalization have taken its place, continuing the attack on the market economy, typically with no reflection on the historical failure of the communist enterprise. It is therefore more than a coincidence that antiglobalization became a popular ideology only once the bipolar world of the cold war came to a definitive end: it has filled the space that Communism vacated.

Antiglobalization, as post-Communist anticapitalism, re-stages the antagonism between political and economics actors (i.e., between the state and the market, reflecting alternative orientations toward geographic space). The components of globalization, especially more cost-efficient transportation and communication, involve capabilities to reduce the relative importance of spatial location. The global economy is therefore marked by the heightened mobility of goods, information, wealth, and labor. In contrast, political power is classically sedentary. It has traditionally been exercised through particular political units (i.e., states), which are defined in territorial terms. This spatiality of political power is not only a modern phenomenon; on the contrary, it reflects the nature of power and force in the human condition altogether. However, the priority of territorial identity took on an amplified importance in the modern age with its emphasis on the nation-state and the derivation of sovereignty from the people as defined in residential terms. Democracy derives its legitimacy from the will of the people inhabiting an area ruled by the state. This spatialization of political power stands at odds with the transgressive mobility associated with trade, in particular, and globalization more broadly. The critique of globalization therefore involves an effort to reassert the primacy of territory over exchange and of the state over economy. The formula is surely not the same as the erstwhile communist model of the nationalization of private property, but it does imply homologous efforts to maintain and strengthen regimes of regulation, as opposed to deregulation, and therefore to restrict aspects of free trade. Antiglobalization advocates the reassertion of the power of the state against the freedom of the market.

Yet this characterization of antiglobalization as the post-Communist form of anticapitalism only catches one dimension, the debate over economic policies, which is frequently overshadowed by other more subjective and affectively charged issues. In other words, the discourse of antiglobalization is arguably less the consequence of the acceleration of international trade and more the product of certain political, rather than economic, shifts. For what is at stake is not only the collapse of communism as an economic paradigm but the corollary emergence of the United States as the one political and military superpower. The rise of American power of course began much earlier, at the latest in the era of the First World War, but its significance only became fully clear with the end of the cold war and the disappearance of any credible challenge to American primacy. Antiglobalization, strictly speaking, may entail an economic protest (no matter how dubious the economics) against capitalism, but in practice, it is inseparable from hostility to the spread of American political influence as well.

In many instances, anticapitalism and anti-Americanism are indistinguishable in the discourse of antiglobalization, except that anti-Americanism typically includes hostility to American foreign policy and cultural influence that may not be directly associated with economic matters, narrowly defined. The economic critique of globalization is heuristically separable from other elements; in practice, the economic campaign against inadequate labor conditions in third world factories is closely intertwined with ecological advocacy for the Kyoto Treaty, human-rights concerns about indigenous peoples, feminist support for women's rights, and the legalistic expansion of institutions of international governance (such as the International Criminal Court). In this diverse and multi-issue field of international protest, in which anticapitalism and anti-Americanism overlap, many ideological components play important roles.

Of particular concern is a disproportionate focus on Israel and Palestine, accorded attention far beyond that given other local conflicts (e.g., Chechnya, Kashmir, Kurdistan, or Tibet). Anticapitalism has always carried some messy intellectual baggage, including a predisposition to associate capitalism and Judaism. In the context of American support for Israel, a virulent strand of antisemitism has developed that further complicates the antiglobalization discourse. Antiglobalization, in other words, is embedded in a strange political culture that combines anti-Americanism, anticapitalism, and antisemitism, along with a generalized resistance to modernity and the free market.

In order to understand this potent mix of ideological currents, it is helpful to look at two key intellectual and literary exponents of this diffuse development. Neither the French sociologist Jean Baudrillard nor the Indian author Arundhati Roy is, strictly speaking, a leader of the antiglobalization movement (although Roy in fact is quite engaged as an activist opposing large dam-building projects in India). For our purposes here, the key is not their specific positions on particular political issues but rather the larger worldview that they convey and its symptomatic standing for the nature of antiglobalization, as it overlaps with anti-Americanism.

Jean Baudrillard and the Protest against Uniformity

The philosophical agenda of antiglobalization involves the defense of multiplicity as against domination by a uniform power, of plurality as against singularity. The movement itself has a pluralistic appearance. Antiglobalization involves advocacy for multiple issues, each with its own legitimacy, local significance, and moral standing. Yet in fact this diversity of positions quickly succumbs to the process of homogenization: antiglobalization rapidly imposes a global logic, a uniform one-size-fits-all argument, onto the multiplicity of different claims. In other words, the protest movement ends up reproducing the same totalizing logic that it has projected onto its adversary. The result is the paranoid vision of a totalizing opponent—the notion that American power is so great that it is responsible for any mishap in the world—as well as a predisposition toward the internal repression of difference, ambiguity, and debate. The antiglobalization movement is not the Communist Party, but there is little room to deviate from the accepted "line."

This implosion, by which antiglobalization globalizes itself, can be traced particularly clearly in the writings of the French philosopher and social theorist Jean Baudrillard, especially in his generalized account (written after the September 11 attacks) of a battle between singularity and particularity. For Baudrillard, globalization means not only the international expansion of the market but also the spread of the universe of symbols: a merely economic protectionism is therefore hopelessly inadequate against what he designates as semiotic promiscuity. "In cultural terms, it is the promiscuity of all signs and values, in other words, pornography. Because the global diffusion of anything through the network amounts to promiscuity, there is no need for sexual obscenity."[1] The resistance to this symbolic exchange takes on diverse, indeed antagonistic forms; in this sense, Baudrillard recognizes the internal multiplicity of antiglobalization.[2] Yet quickly all resistance is defined as a hostility to the same enemy, and the internal process of homogenization ensues. It becomes the conformism of the nonconformists.

It was, for Baudrillard, September 11 that concretized this inversion: a single, all-encompassing, global logic took over the vision of antiglobalization. The protest movement against uniformity succumbed to its own negative vision. Suddenly, all local strategies of terrorism, with their specific causes and goals, were seen as culminating in the same, all-defining act of terrorism. For Baudrillard, "Terrorism is an act that restores an irreducible particularity in the middle of a generalized exchange system. All particularities (species, individuals, cultures) which today challenge the establishment of global circulation directed by one single power take their revenge and their death through this terrorist transformation of the situation."[3] Not only does Baudrillard—like other European intellectuals discussed in

---

1. Jean Baudrillard, *Power Inferno* (Paris: Galilée, 2002), 67.

2. Cf. ibid., 72.

3. Jean Baudrillard, "The Spirit of Terrorism," trans. Kathy Ackerman, *Telos* 121 (Fall 2001), 135.

chapter 2—thereby provide an explicit defense of terrorism. He
also subsumes all local practices of resistance into the unifying
logic of the one grand terrorist deed. The movement that began
as the advocacy of difference against the empire of sameness
ends up imposing its own sameness on all its components.

One intriguing implication of Baudrillard's claim—that all
local resistance to globalization was already inherent in the September 11 attacks—is that the allegedly extensive international
expressions of solidarity in the immediate aftermath of the
attacks, the protestations of compassion and identification with
the United States, may have been less than sincere, perhaps even
only superficial and perfunctory. The discussion of public opinion data in chapter 1 corroborates this claim. One can conclude
that the turn of European opinion against the United States in
the subsequent year, particularly in regard to the Iraq war, had
less to do with the alleged diplomatic failures of the Bush
administration than with an ambiguity inherent in those initial
expressions of sympathy, which were never very far from the
accusation that the attacks were actually deserved. For our purposes here, however, what is more important than the slide in
European public opinion is the question of how antiglobalization globalizes itself into a single logic, undermining its original
multiplicity.

A single world power is cast in an apocalyptic struggle with
a singularized opposition: two omnipresent agents in a Mani-
chean paranoia. There is no longer any particularity that stands
outside the all-consuming global antagonism, and consequently,
no individuality either. The anxiety of the government security
apparatus that terrorists may lurk anywhere is actually quite
moderate when contrasted with the mentality of the protest
movement, the persecution complex of the globalization-critics.
They rigorously ascribe all evil to the United States and its cap-

italism: nothing is beyond American power, nothing beyond American control, no misfortune for which American capitalism is not guilty.)

Meanwhile, the critics of globalization claim for themselves the moral superiority derived from the position of underdevelopment: their de facto celebration of backwardness is taken as the foundation for a critique of civilization. The contrast with all ideologies of progress, even including classical Marxism, is quite clear. For Marxists, backwardness only meant poverty; for the opponents of globalization, backwardness is imagined to be the guarantor of genuine intelligence and ethical judgment. Ultimately, this represents a late version of the romantic fascination with "the noble savage." Baudrillard casts this superior primitive as a terrorist, while Roy, as we will see, ends up in the celebration of indigenous culture and hostility to the West.

For Baudrillard, antiglobalization, including terrorism, is the result of globalized modernity, not in the obvious sense that globalization may provoke resistance among its victims but in the sense that the totalizing system itself yearns for its own destruction. Terrorism is not, he argues, the result of some exterior force that opposes modernization but "the verdict and the sentence that this society directs at itself."[4] This claim is fully consistent with Baudrillard's more extreme formulation with regard to September 11 that there is "a terrorist imagination in all of us. . . . Basically, they did it, but we wanted it."[5] In both cases, his argument involves claiming that antiglobalization, even in its most destructive form, does not come from the outside but expresses the self-destructive desire of modernity itself. As a theoretician of antiglobalization, however, what he dem-

---

4. Baudrillard, *Power Inferno*, 83.
5. Baudrillard, "The Spirit of Terrorism," 134.

onstrates in fact is the opposite: the manner in which diverse cultural positions or singularities dissolve into a generalized movement driven by the paranoid vision of an undifferentiated and inescapable market. In other words, the pathological projection is not, as Baudrillard claims, the result of modernity but rather, the characteristic perspective of the critics of globalization, who fantasize conspiracies and contamination everywhere. Capitalism becomes the pandemic against which local virtue must protect itself by resisting promiscuity. Baudrillard's identification of this anxiety regarding semiotic contamination is useful in explaining the moment of sexual repression in antiglobalization—the reluctance to criticize the Taliban is evidence on this point—and betrays the repressive and xenophobic predisposition in the movement, the fear of contact with the foreign. This outcome is particularly clear in the next example.

Arundhati Roy and the Fear of the Foreign

Baudrillard himself typically maintains a scholarly and sociological distance from his material. Even while attacking the homogenizing power of global capitalism, in a way that is clearly directed against the United States, his anti-Americanism remains muffled and camouflaged by the conventions and forms of a generalizing and abstract social theory. His essays represent the cool end of the spectrum of the rhetorical registers of antiglobalization.

The writings of Arundhati Roy present a strikingly different model. To be sure, Roy's account resembles Baudrillard's to the extent that both elaborate a worldview that links an antidevelopmental cult of backwardness to strident antiglobalization: maintaining the local becomes a universal program. Yet Roy displays none of Baudrillard's conceptual abstraction and objective tone. Instead of scholarly distance, her critique of globalization grows shrill, and her anti-Americanism takes on an urgent ring. For this reason, the essays she has written as a public intellectual have been criticized for the lack of serious substance, and the political effect of her role in protest movements has been subject to skeptical scrutiny. Nonetheless, the character of her discourse—rather than the substance of her claims and arguments—is of interest in this context, since it illuminates some features of the affect and projections associated with antiglobalization. Why does anti-Americanism as antiglobalization sometimes sound fanatic?

Roy earned international acclaim with her novel *The God of Small Things*, which won the Booker Prize in 1997. (A critic of globalization, she nonetheless belongs to the growing group of celebrity authors who address a global readership and who are not easily categorized in traditional national-literary terms.) Building on her literary success, she launched herself on a second career as a political activist, writing polemical essays against India's big dam-building projects and the nuclear bomb ("The Cost of Living," 1999), and against the globalization of the energy industry (*Power Politics*, 2001). Critics on the left have questioned the integrity of her positions, suggesting that it is more her celebrity status than her engagement that is at stake; critics on the right have properly queried her consistent anti-westernism.[6] Yet aside from the ambiguities of her political position, her writing is noteworthy insofar as the style itself testifies to underlying predispositions: her own and, hypothetically, those of the movement against globalization more broadly. By

---

6. Ramachandra Guha, "The Arun Shourie of the Left," *The Hindu* Nov. 26, 2000; Ian Buruma, "The Anti-American," *The New Republic Online*, March 17, 2003, http://www.tnr.com.

looking closely at Roy's writings, we can inquire into the character of antiglobalization.

Roy's public discourse tends to replace reasoned argument with affective performance. Indeed she frequently makes emotional responses her topic, rather than the phenomena that elicit those responses. She simultaneously flaunts an exaggerated affect of her own. Thus, for example, in the midst of an otherwise expository essay, she breaks out into the cry ". . . hear the thrumming, the deadly drumbeat of burgeoning anger. Please. Please, stop the war now."[7] In this case she is referring to the Afghanistan war and the erroneous expectation that it would elicit enormous resistance, leading to a disastrous outcome comparable to that of the Soviet invasion. Yet the issue here is not that she was wrong in this particular instance (as she may be in others). What is remarkable is her stylistic readiness to shift out of a modicum of rational debate into an overwrought language of direct address, threat, and exaggeration. She allows her writing to become so emotional, however, because her analysis is itself focused on questions of affective response: she is less concerned with facts or political processes than with sentiments and psychological predispositions. Her ultimate topic is subjectivity, and she addresses it in a subjective manner. Thus we find her dwelling on the "prevailing paranoia," and the "raging emotions [that] are being let loose into the world."[8] It follows then that she characterizes the U.S. population not in terms of any imaginable analysis of political interests or traditions—its attitudes are not taken that seriously—or in terms of political parties or competing candidates but solely as the victim of an emotional manipulation. Political slogans "are cynically doled

7. Arundhati Roy, *Power Politics* (Cambridge: South End Press, 2001), 140.
8. Ibid., 139.

out by government spokesmen like a daily dose of vitamins or anti-depressants. Regular medication ensures that mainland America continues to remain the enigma it has always been—a curiously insular people, administered by a pathologically med-dlesome promiscuous government."[9] This fear of promiscuity, already identified in Baudrillard's account, will recur in our reading of Roy. The discourse of antiglobalization seems to be carried by the imagery of contamination. For now, suffice it to note this congruence of hypersubjectivism and anti-American-ism. The enormous threat that she imagines America to pose is not substantiated in political terms, where it might be debated; it is turned instead into emotion and affect.

As with other critics of U.S. foreign policy, Roy refuses to ask whether there might be some rationality in the U.S. political consensus. Instead, she resorts to the thesis of a totally manipu-lated public, driven by emotion and devoid of reason. Emotion trumps argument, but this verdict that she directs at the Ameri-can public is in fact an appropriate characterization of her own speech. Hence the relative absence of any economic theory (which might have been expected in the discussion of major economic phenomena) and the curious confusion of categories in the political discussion: she can never quite explain if she is arguing for more state regulation of the economy or for less state bureaucracy in order to diminish corruption. She rarely gets to this point of clarification, and her refusal to develop rational argument drives a further prominent feature of her essayistic prose: the stylistic preference for rhetorical questions, indeed, frequently the string of rhetorical questions—a gesture that allows her to pretend that she possesses a simple answer, which others ought to know already, while absolving her of an obli-

9. Ibid., 144.

gation to divulge the presumed answer and defend it with argument. This series of questions therefore amounts to a rhetoric of arrogance, the goal of which is presumably to counterfeit a logical high ground, but the result is the constant demonstration of the limits of her thinking. Even positively predisposed and well-meaning readers can only be disappointed by her constant refusal to follow through on a line of argument.

Her writing displays a marked preference for blanket dismissiveness and innuendo. References to the free press or the free market are placed in quotation marks, to indicate denigration, without ever elaborating on the problem suggested: an easy way to convey a hostile stance without accepting the responsibility of explaining why she thinks a free press and a free market are not desirable institutions. Similarly, she has a propensity to indicate the policies she opposes by personalizing them, associating them with typically unnamed figures whom she briefly describes in derogatory ways, a strategy designed to establish a cozy relationship of prejudice with her reader. As discussed in chapter 3, she conjures up at one point "a marrowy American panelist" at a conference; no other panelist is described, nor is any member of another nation given this sort of physical presence.[10] In a separate passage, another American is described as "rolling his R's in his North American way," as if having an accent were the crime.[11] More important than her claims regarding the policies she opposes—and these claims never even rise to the level of coherent argument—is this strategy to personalize and demean her opponent rhetorically: as if the pronunciation or the body type alone were sufficient grounds to reject the stance associated with anonymous Ameri-

10. Ibid., 41.
11. Ibid., 36.

can individuals. Her rhetorical success, however, lies precisely in her propagandistic ability to establish this anti-American bond with her readers: not based on policy debate but through hostile caricatures of accent and physical appearance.

This direction of animosity toward individuals because of physical appearance, accent, and nationality is an expression of the strategy of stereotyping and racialization that pervades Roy's prose in multiple ways. In some cases, it is quite pronounced and polemical. Thus, for example, in her attack on the Indian development of nuclear weapons, she deftly redirects the reader's anger away from India or the Indian government that developed the weapon and toward the presumed real culprit: the white race. "[Nuclear weapons] are purveyors of madness. They are the ultimate colonizer. Whiter than any white man that ever lived. The very heart of whiteness."[12] The Indian nuclear arsenal is, apparently, not the fault of the Indian government but of the westerners who invented the weapons. Indeed she not only insists that it was the West, (i.e., the United States) that initiated the nuclear arms race, but she also goes on to make nuclear weaponry identical with a racial enemy: it is the opponent's corporeal difference that elicits hatred. Hence her explicit condemnation of the West: "These are people whose histories are spongy with the blood of others. . . . They have plundered nations, snuffed out civilizations, exterminated entire populations."[13] One looks in vain for nuance in the judgment; instead one finds the blanket condemnation of the white West (as if the West were solely white) as a whole, which stands as a universal and ineluctable threat.

12. Arundhati Roy, *The Cost of Living* (New York: Modern Library, 1999), 101.
13. Ibid., 112.

The only alternative, for Roy, seems to lie in the idealized self-sufficiency of the village past.[14] Absolute identity, without foreign presence, without external exchange, and without modernization, amounts to the antiglobal utopia, and it stands in contrast to the infinite threats associated with the outside world. This infinite menace, exuded by the all-powerful West, takes the form of the all-destructive bomb and assaults mind and body in what is ultimately the expression of a paranoid worldview: unlimited danger is always everywhere. The only possible safety is in a retreat to the absolute origin of undifferentiation.

This worldview, the search for an absolute self-identity and the rejection of outside forces as always only destructive, finds its fullest expression in Roy's novel *The God of Small Things*. Although the book does touch on some political matters— Indian Communism, the labor movement, the relationship to colonialism—it is not primarily a tendentious or explicitly engaged novel; it therefore stands at odds with Roy's polemical essays, which are very much directed toward a political public sphere. In particular, it would be difficult to say that *The God of Small Things* takes an explicit position on globalization, except perhaps in the peripheral denigration of tourism; this, however, is only a minor part of the novel. Nonetheless, as a whole it is in fact driven by a logic that corroborates the antiglobalization of Roy's engagement elsewhere and that therefore can serve as a further indication of the tendencies and pressures at stake in the critique of globalization. On multiple levels, one finds the constant celebration of indigenous nativist substance and the corollary denunciation of all that is foreign. The strident antiwesternism and the hatred of whiteness evidenced in her essays are very much compatible with the substance of the novel.

14. Ibid., 53.

In terms of aesthetic culture, two key events structure the work: the fictional family's visit to a cinema to see *The Sound of Music* and a performance of traditional Indian kathakali dance. The former scene turns into a site of depravity—not the film itself, but the foyer of the theater where the young boy is molested. Roy depicts modernity, at least the modernity of Western cinema, as the site of perversion. In contrast, kathakali is presented as the opposite of tourism, the source of a cultural authenticity that opposes the forms of the Western culture industry. Roy conveys an aesthetic program of familiarity and community—precisely the antipode to cinematic suspense: "It didn't matter that the story had begun, because kathakali discovered long ago that the secret of the Great Stories is that they *have* no secrets. The Great Stories are the ones you have heard and want to hear again."[15] The organic communalism of traditional dance performance is mobilized as an alternative to touristic commercialism and to the degradation of entertainment cinema. The move is reminiscent of other celebrations of oral cultures in literary criticism, in particular, the literary critic Walter Benjamin's suggested opposition between story-telling and novel-writing.[16] Yet while Benjamin emphasized the moment of community as an alternative to a lonely and isolated individuality, Roy pushes the model in another direction, toward the assertion of the positive value of familiarity. Her point is not community, or—more bluntly—collectivized communalism, as for Benjamin, but the maintenance of a pure homogeneity. Her cultural program is a return: to that which is not foreign, to family and the familiar, a return ultimately to native soil and

15. Arundhati Roy, *The God of Small Things* (New York: Harper, 1998), 218.
16. Cf. Walter Benjamin, "The Storyteller," in *Illuminations*, ed. Hannah Arendt (New York: Schocken, 1968), 83–110.

native blood. Her critique of globalization turns into the fear of the foreign.

As a whole, the plot of the novel therefore necessarily involves a return to the native village. In terms of the family structure that organizes the fiction, the erotic relations between Indians and Western foreigners all end in failure. *The God of Small Things* might easily, and appropriately, be read as a denunciation of miscegenation. The novel suggests that the whiteness that Roy otherwise condemns is incompatible with the Indian body. This sexualized xenophobia draws attention to how a typically left-wing antiglobalization sentiment can overlap with a sometimes right-wing hostility to immigration, since both are concerned with the integrity of borders. In Roy's novel, Rahel's brief marriage to an American is particularly insipid and short-lived, while Chacko's marriage to an Englishwoman ends in divorce, and their only child drowns. In a moment of particular cruelty, the novel concludes with a sexualized humiliation of the bereaved mother. Other encounters with the West are similarly degraded, including a dalliance between the aunt and a Catholic priest. Throughout the novel, moreover, tourism corrupts: the son of a Communist figure, bearing the name "Lenin," fears that this nomenclature may offend Western foreigners and therefore masquerades as "Levin." The Jewish name is associated with the West and represents a humorously diminutive contrast to the threatening revolutionary reference "Lenin." The antisemitism of this labeling lies in the suggestion of inferiority, the presentation of the Jewish name as meek in contrast to the heroic "Lenin." Meanwhile the Anglophilia of the central family remains the novel's major problem. Apparently, for Roy, nothing good ever came of study abroad or foreign spouses.

Although foreignness is the problem, the solution lies in the search for an absolute local identity: this is the cultural program that mirrors antiglobalization. The colonial mentality of yearning for Britain gives way to a new feeling of being at home in India. Yet for Roy, this goes far beyond decolonization. That search for identity leads to the novel's culmination in the incestuous love of the two twins, Rahel and Esta—a desire for endogamy as Roy's extreme expression of the fear of globalization. Promiscuity (Baudrillard's problem too, as we have seen) evidently includes any marrying outside of the native culture. In contrast, the love affair with Indian culture, staged particularly in the kathakali dance, betrays a narcissism that culminates in self-love, the corollary to which is the hatred of the other. Hence, the contempt for the outside world, the disdain for Anglophilia, and the requirement that the novel kill off the half-breed child of the mixed marriage. No family ties between England and India are allowed to survive as the children of mixed relations die off. Hence also the historical frame that is placed analytically around the novel's investigation. The problem, so the narrator asserts, began long before the plot itself: ". . . it actually began thousands of years ago. Long before the Marxists came. Before the British took Malabar, before the Dutch Ascendency" and so forth. Indeed the claim is made that it preceded all such imperialism and "that it really began in the days when the Love Laws were made. The laws that lay down who should be loved and how. And how much."[17] To be sure, the chronology does not erase the imperialist legacy for Roy, but an original sin precedes all such occupations. The "laws of love" pertain to prohibitions of love across castes—the affair between the protagonist Ammu, and the untouchable Velutha—but also the taboo against incest. The latter is at the core of the logic: the anthropological mandate to exogamy generates a

17. Roy, *The God of Small Things*, 33.

pressure to disrupt original identity, and the resistance to that pressure turns into the paranoid fear of the exterior and of foreignness. Hostility to the outside is the indirect expression of erotic attraction to the other, which has to be suppressed. Roy's novel has the advantage of making clear the psychological and cultural forces at operation in the mentality of antiglobalization and its proximity to xenophobia.

Theodor Adorno:
On the Inappropriateness of Anti-Americanism

Baudrillard and Roy seem to present different accounts of antiglobalization. For Baudrillard, it is a matter of opposition to the force of total uniformity; for Roy, a nationalistic resentment against foreignness. Yet these are ultimately just two sides of the same coin, linked moreover to a generalized resentment against modernization, development, and capitalism. Anti-Americanism is the result. In order to sort through some of these issues, it is helpful to turn to an older tradition, the "Critical Theory" of the Frankfurt School, especially the writings of the German philosopher Theodor Adorno. Classical Critical Theory was nothing if not an inquiry into the genealogy of fanaticism as a political and social-psychological phenomenon, both with regard to the virulence of fascist movements in the 1930s and to aspects of student movements in the 1960s. For all the obvious differences, there were deep similarities, particularly in the overlap of anti-Americanism and hostility to modernization.

Before approaching Adorno's cultural judgments, it is important to point out some undeniable limitations of Critical Theory, especially with regard to globalization and other objective social and economic processes. The Frankfurt School inherited many of Marxism's failings, especially an underdeveloped interest in the institutional relationship of the state to the market; descriptions of social processes were based primarily on ideological claims and the political program, rather than on empirical observation or genuine data. In particular, the question of the relationship between the political and economic sectors of modern society was treated with enormous oversimplification. For classical Marxism, there was ultimately no separate political or public sphere, since state action was treated as always mirroring ruling class economic interest: hence the predisposition to propose deterministic accounts of society and an inability to address questions of practice, at least in mainstream Marxism. If one assumes that everything is only economics, there is little room for independent political considerations.

However, this reductionist treatment of politics as merely economics in disguise took on a new color during the second third of the twentieth century, marked as it was by various examples of massive state intervention in the economy. It is tempting to venture the claim that the expansive state of the era of National Socialism and Stalinism was a serendipitous topic for Critical Theory's Marxism, since in those instances, the opportunity to distinguish between market and state was in fact minimal. The older Marxist vice of treating the political sphere as the direct function of economics suddenly turned into a virtue in an era in which state intervention in the economy had expanded enormously. In this context of extensive state regulation (in totalitarian regimes, of course, much more than in Western, democratic welfare states, but there as well), the question of the distinction between state and market became less pronounced. Just as classical nineteenth-century Marxism had had little to say about the state or the specificity of politics, early twentieth-century Critical Theory had even less to say about the specificity of economics. In any case, this intellectual history

clearly demonstrates the limits of the pertinence of Critical Theory to the objective economic discussion of globalization, be it
with regard to the empirical processes of political economy or
the policy questions associated with regulation and deregulation.

However, while Critical Theory has little to contribute to
empirical social-scientific analysis or economic policy (but of
course neither do the competing models of cultural theory, neo-
Marxism and post-structuralism, at the beginning of the twenty-
first century), it is nonetheless useful in the interrogation of the
overlapping fields of antiglobalization and anti-Americanism.
Our terrain of inquiry therefore shifts from the primary question
of globalization as the economic consequence of the international market in goods and services to another set of issues: the
cultural consequences of globalization and, in particular, the
emergence of the prominent and complex discourse of
antiglobalization.

Why has antiglobalization taken the place of Communist
anticapitalism? If globalization in fact produces so much wealth,
why does it elicit so much opposition? Or more pointedly: how
and why does antiglobalization inherit the hostility to modernization that has motivated earlier protest movements? Such a
rejection is often associated with stereotypical anti-Americanism
and frequently with antisemitism as well. Approaching the globalization debate as a cultural rather than an economic matter
invites an analysis parallel to the cultural criticism of Nazism
carried out by Critical Theory. The framework of this essay is
too narrow to reconstruct the full range of the Frankfurt
School's accounts of fascism and antisemitism, or even their
sparse comments on the state and economy. Still it is illuminating to contrast some of Adorno's more pointed analyses, espe-

cially in the volume *Stichworte* (Catchwords),[18] with the paradigmatic critiques of globalization exemplified by the writings of Baudrillard and Roy. What does Critical Theory suggest with regard to the particular psychology of antiglobalization? The question is pertinent because the discontent with modernity that Critical Theory identified in fascism and antisemitism has reappeared today in the movement against globalization.

Published in 1969, *Stichworte* was the last volume of Adorno's work that he was able to oversee before his death, and it includes some of the seminal analyses on the intersection of politics and culture. At the center of the volume are three essays that define his legacy with regard to our current concerns: the standing of national identity, the relationship of Germany and Europe to the United States, and the question of postfascist culture. Frankfurt School thinking revolves particularly around the last point: a judgment on the possibilities of culture and politics in the wake of National Socialism and the Holocaust. The essay "Education after Auschwitz" puts forward both a fragmentary social psychology of the mentality that supported the Nazi regime and a program for a pedagogy against cruelty. Although classical and orthodox Marxism, from which Critical Theory diverged, emphasized claims about the so-called developmental laws of capitalism and Lenin's theory of revolution, Adorno was concerned with the failure of revolutionary projects, the paradoxical motivation of populations to support fascism, and their attraction to opting against freedom. How can we explain the attraction exercised by brutality, domination, and tyrannical authority? His answers are in many ways framed by his own

18. Theodor W. Adorno, *Critical Models: Interventions and Catchwords*, trans. Henry W. Pickford (New York: Columbia University Press, 1998). This volume includes translations of the two separate German volumes named in the subtitle.

historical context, the experience of the Hitler regime, the growing knowledge of the terror of Stalinism, and his encounter with the mass-cultural democracy of the United States of the 1940s. Yet what remains particularly compelling is his criticism of underlying processes of forced collectivism and his corollary identification of the antidote in an insistence on autonomous individuality. Adorno's dialectic of individuality and collectivism, forged in the statist and Fordist era of the midcentury, takes on a renewed urgency in the context of late twentieth-century debates between neoliberalism and antiglobal anticapitalism.

Consider Adorno's diagnosis of the capacity of individuals to participate in the persecution of others. Formulated with direct reference to the Holocaust, his explanation does not involve assertions of long-standing prejudice, tragic flaws in German culture, or the sort of allegedly atavistic ethnic hatred with which journalists glossed the wars in the Balkans. Instead, he describes a modern social psychology. The overarching integration of society, a forced conformism like the Nazi *Gleichschaltung*, the consolidation of institutional power under Hitler, undermines the vitality of local institutions and individual personalities. Free space for free people dwindles away. "The pressure exerted by the prevailing universal on everything particular, upon the individual people and the individual institutions, has a tendency to destroy the particular and the individual together with their power of resistance. With the loss of their identity and power of resistance, people also forget those qualities by virtue of which they are able to pit themselves against what at some moment might lure them again to commit atrocity. Perhaps they are hardly able to offer resistance when the established authorities once again give them the order, so long as it is in the name of some ideal in which they half or not at all believe."[19] The collectivization of society (i.e., the massive expansion of the state into previously unregulated spheres of social life) weakens local identity structures, which then become ever more susceptible to a renewed participation in brutality: it becomes all the more likely that one will just follow orders. In other words, a general, nearly inescapable so-called rationalization of society is the precondition for unreasonable and irrational behavior. The more everything falls under some central control, the more civilization declines. For Adorno, the civilizing ability of society depends above all on the particularity of individuals rather than on the framing institutions of social control. Human accomplishments result from individual integrity, not from normative regulation. However, as the collectivizing state subverts the integrity of individuals—for Adorno a historical process, the inexorable inevitability of which he surely overstated in a way that, in retrospect, seems typical for mid-twentieth-century critics of a conformist modernity—individuals lose the power to resist invitations to take part in cruelty. Understanding how to promote such a resistance is, for Adorno, the sine qua non of any "education after Auschwtiz." The real alternative to totalitarianism is individual integrity.

For our purposes, it is important to determine how Adorno's insistence on individualism as the vehicle for resistance to conformism can be mapped onto the terrain of globalization and antiglobalization. The alternative to conformism (the consequence of an expansive state) is not some better conformism but rather the opposite: a strengthened individuality and the consistent rejection of all collectivisms. "I think the most important way to confront the danger of a recurrence [of Auschwitz] is to work against the brute predominance of all collectives, to

19. Ibid., 193–194.

intensify the resistance to it by concentrating on the problem of collectivization. That is not as abstract as it sounds in view of the passion with which especially young and progressively minded people desire to integrate themselves into something or other."[20] Protest movements, in other words, may just reproduce the conformism against which they seemed to be opposed. For Adorno, the solution does not lie in the assertion of a minority group identity against a majority identity, or even in the evocation of a collective solidarity with a suffering group. Collectivized solidarity, on the contrary, is—owing to its collectivism—antithetical to human compassion, which depends instead on the possibility of individual sensibility. The best way to work against a repetition of Auschwitz is to oppose collectivist mentalities and the structures, be they political, cultural, or psychological, that support them.

Adorno's Critical Theory is significant for contemporary discussions in two distinct ways. First, it entails the critique of a blind activism. Even admirable ideals can be discredited by their flawed pursuit; the ends do not justify the means. His criticism of the West German student movement of the 1960s remains relevant to aspects of the antiglobalization movement and its propensity to engage in street violence and vandalism, as became clear in the riots in Seattle and Genoa. Second, with regard to the problem of a homogenizing collectivism, Adorno's vision tilts very much toward the defense of the individual against the state—and is hence objectively neoliberal, no matter how anachronistic that term may be for the analysis of Adorno in his historical context. The logic of Adorno's critique of totalitarianism implies the desideratum of a smaller state, not expanded regulation: more individualistic entrepreneurs, fewer

20. Ibid., 197.

regulatory agencies. This however suggests that his thinking is orthogonal to the central motif of antiglobalization, the appeal for greater regulation of the market, be it in the form of "local" protectionism or through international bureaucracies and agreements. In the end, the defense of autonomy and particularity means that Adorno's implied economic theory—despite his Marxist background—is closer to Hayek than to Stiglitz.

Adorno's defense of individualism against collectivism pervades the following two essays in *Stichworte*, which should be read in relation to each other: "On the Question: What Is German" and "Scientific Experiences of a European Scholar in America." The two texts convey Adorno's complex relations to both German and American culture, marked by the characteristic ambivalence of affection for and critique of each. The two essays, read together, explore the antinomies of modern culture, the philosophical humanities that define Adorno's German world, and the empirical social science of the United States. As is well known, Adorno remained deeply critical of that empiricism, and he was always more at home in the world of German speculative thought than in modern quantitative social science. His unexpectedly warm account of his American experience is, therefore, even more striking. His evaluation of America pertains to the globalization discussion to the extent that the latter is largely about the United States and an anti-Americanism that Adorno, for all his high-culture mandarinism, never endorsed. In other words, Adorno had all the European high-cultural biases that might have made him an elitist anti-American; instead, however, he expressed approval for American culture and denounced the German anti-Americanism of the 1960s.

Yet even more important than deciphering his particular judgment on the United States or Europe is identifying the underlying rationale. Anglo-American individualism, he suggests, generated a greater capacity to resist fascism than was ever the case in continental Europe. Continental Europe, in contrast, remained deeply defined by a culture of authoritarianism. (He does not distinguish much within Europe, unfortunately; nonetheless, the distinction between European culture on the one hand, and the Anglo-American world on the other, repeats the polarity we could observe in Brecht's wartime reflections discussed in chapter 3.) Hence his analyses of the German predisposition to dismiss or even denounce American culture as too superficial, commercial, or insignificant. He reaches back to the notorious case of the Germanophile Houston Stewart Chamberlain, who left his native England to marry into the Wagner family. (Adorno's move to explore German nationalism by examining a British expatriate exemplifies Critical Theory's program of de-essentializing national identity: the most voluble German was not really German at all.) Chamberlain's hostile judgment on Anglo-American culture, characteristically racialized in the form of antisemitism, is—for Adorno, the Marxist—the effect not of a genuinely different social model, not of an authentic distinction between two national traditions, but rather of a relative underdevelopment within the fundamentally identical process of economic modernization. Germans, or a Germanophile like Chamberlain, could celebrate continental Europe against the commercialism of England only because the continental economy was relatively, if only minimally, backward. It would soon catch up, but in the meantime the apparent distinction in the degree of commercialism could be misunderstood to indicate profound cultural distinctions. The result of this economic backwardness was the antimodernist and antisemitic populist discourse of German cultural superiority over Anglo-American commercialism.

Adorno rejects that European ideology, especially its reductionist account of a merely venal Anglo-American world. On the contrary, he associates American advanced capitalism emphatically with an aspiration to freedom that, so he claims, takes on a practical character in real-world efforts to promote freedom, in contrast to the merely philosophical freedom of continental philosophy: "Following a tradition of hostility to civilization that is older than Spengler, one feels superior to the other continent because it has produced nothing but refrigerators and automobiles while Germany produced the culture of the spirit. . . . In America, however, in the omnipresent for-other all the way to *keep smiling,* there also flourishes sympathy, compassion, and commiseration with the lot of the weaker. The energetic will to establish a free society—rather than only apprehensively thinking of freedom and, even in thought, degrading it into voluntary submission—does not forfeit its goodness because the societal system imposes limits on its realization. In Germany, arrogance toward America is inappropriate."[21] The impropriety of that arrogance is not primarily about the history of the Second World War or the notion of some obligatory gratitude for the American defense of West Germany during the cold war. For Adorno, the issue is rather the difference between the American culture of freedom, on the one hand, and the German, or more broadly European, regime of regulatory statism, on the other. Adorno's politics are consistent on this point. This is why he has long been rejected by the German Left for his anticollectivism and by the German nationalist Right for his pro-Americanism. Not only his positive judgment on the United States but, more important, his philosophical admonition against collectivized identity structures help clarify the ideology of antiglobalization, just as they shed useful light on the growing difference

21. Ibid., 210.

in values between continental Europe and the United States, the end of the so-called community of values, the allegedly shared ideals that united the United States and Western Europe in the cold war transatlantic alliance.

This is not the place to try to make sense of all the tensions within Adorno's thought, especially the balancing act between his Marxist legacy and his anti-Communism. That constellation of ideas is, to say the least, complex. For our purposes here, however, it suffices to note that several of the predominant motifs in some of Adorno's work retain relevance in the face of antiglobalization: the defense of American individualism against European collectivism, the suspicion of regimes of statist regulation, a skepticism toward the conformist group identities in activist youth movements (regardless of their ideals), and a wariness of the prominent antisemitism in antimodernist protest movements. The point is certainly not that all these characteristics recur uniformly throughout the antiglobalization movement but that they recur with enough frequency to be worrisome. In this sense Adorno's analysis of fascist and postfascist antimodernism—the point at which the "authoritarian personality" recurs in the presumably antiauthoritarian protest movement—has significance for the understanding of contemporary antiglobalization and its anti-American message.

Critical Theory's historical analysis of fascism and authoritarian predispositions in the past—the antimodernism of fascism or the 1960s counterculture—is certainly not the same as the critical-theoretical consideration of antiglobalization today. The differences in context are significant. Yet the understanding of historical fascism as an anticapitalist and antimodernist protest with cultural and psychological corollaries suggests parallels to the ideological texture of contemporary antiglobalization sentiment: the fear of the free market, the anxiety about mobility, the celebration of indigenousness, and the totalizing fear of an external threat. Whatever the progressive pretenses of antiglobalization, its repressive potential is clear. Antiglobalization is deeply fearful of freedom and therefore becomes hostile to the institutions and symbols of freedom. The conclusion to draw from these observations is not that it is wrong or impossible to criticize aspects of the international economy. On the contrary, neither Baudrillard nor Roy appears to have given serious attention to the international economy and its consequences. What their writings nonetheless demonstrate are some of the problematic dynamics that operate in the culture of antiglobalization and that explain its turn toward anti-Americanism. Adorno's critique of anti-Americanism and his analysis of the cultural consequences of collectivism shed important light on these features of anti-globalization today.

Bibliography ❧

Aburish, Said K. *Saddam Hussein: The Politics of Revenge.* London: Bloomsbury, 2000.

Addison, Joseph. "The Campaign, A Poem to His Grace the Duke of Marlborough, 1705. *The Penn State Archive of Samuel Johnson's Lives of Poets*, ed. Kathleen Nulton Kemmerer. http://www.hn.psu.edu.faculty/kkemmerer/poets/addison/campaign.htm.

Adorno, Theodor W. *Critical Models: Interventions and Catchwords.* Trans. Henry W. Pickford. New York: Columbia University Press, 1998.

Al-Khalil, Samir [Kanan Makiya, pseud.]. *The Monument: Art, Vulgarity and Responsibility in Iraq.* Berkeley: University of California Press, 1991.

Arendt, Hannah. *The Origins of Totalitarianism.* New York: Harcourt, 1968.

Baudrillard, Jean. *Power Inferno.* Paris: Galilée, 2002.

———. "The Spirit of Terrorism." Trans. Kathy Ackerman. *Telos* 121 (Fall 2001): 134–42.

Benjamin, Walter. "The Storyteller." In *Illuminations*, trans. Harry Zohn, ed. Hannah Arendt. New York: Schocken, 1968.

Berman, Russell A. *Cultural Studies of Modern Germany: History, Representation, and Nationhood.* Madison: University of Wisconsin Press, 1993.

Bohrer, Karl Heinz. "Provinzialismus (II): ein Psychogramm." *Merkur* 45, no. 3 (March 1991): 255–61.

Brecht, Bertolt. *Journals, 1934–1955.* Trans. Hugh Rorrison. New York: Routledge, 1996.

Broder, Henryk M. *Kein Krieg, Nirgends: Die Deutschen und der Terror.* Berlin: Berlin Verlag, 2002.

Buruma, Ian. "The Anti-American." *The New Republic Online.* March 17, 2003. http://www.tnr.com.

Bush, George H. W. "Address to the Nation Announcing the Deployment of United States Armed Forces to Saudi Arabia." August 8, 1990.

———. "Remarks to Department of Defense Employees." August 15, 1990.

———. "Remarks at a Republican Campaign Rally in Manchester, New Hampshire." October 23, 1990.

Chicago Council on Foreign Relations and German Marshall Fund of the United States. *Worldviews 2002: Comparing American and European Public Opinion on Foreign Policy.* 2002. http://www.worldviews.org.

Diner, Dan. *America in the Eyes of the Germans: An Essay on Anti-Americanism.* Trans. Allison Brown. Princeton: Markus Wiener, 1996.

Enzensberger, Hans Magnus. "Hitler's Successor: Saddam Hussein in the Context of German History." Trans. Mary Strand. *Telos* 86 (Winter 1990–91): 153–57.

Goethe, Johann Wolfgang. "Wilhelm Meisters Lehrjahre." In: Goethe's *Werke,* Vol. 7., ed. Erich Trunz. Hamburg: Christian Wegner Verlag, 1962.

Guha, Ramachandra. "The Arun Shourie of the Left." *The Hindu* (Madras), November 26, 2000.

Habermas, Jürgen, et al. "Das alte Europa antwortet Herrn Rumsfeld." *Frankfurter Allgemeine Zeitung,* January 24, 2003.

Hamza, Khidir. *Saddam's Bombmaker: The Terrifying Story of the Iraqi Nuclear and Biological Weapons Agenda.* New York: Scribner, 2000.

Hitler, Adolf. *Mein Kampf.* Trans. Ralph Manheim. London: Hutchinson, 1969.

Jünger, Ernst. "Der Kampf als inneres Erelbnis." In *Sämtliche Werke, Essays I: Betrachtungen zur Zeit.* Stuttgart: Klett Verlag, 1980.

Kaufman, Robert. "Aura, Still." *October,* no. 99 (Winter 2002): 45–80.

Khadduri, Majid. *Independent Iraq: A Study in Iraqi Politics.* London: Oxford University Press, 1960.

Lukács, Georg. *The Theory of the Novel: A Historico-Philosophical Essay on the Forms of Great Epic Literature.* Trans. Anna Bostock. Cambridge: MIT Press, 1971.

Macaulay, Thomas Babbington. "The Life and Writings of Addison." In Macaulay, *Essays on Milton and Addison.* New York: Longmans, Green, and Co., 1900.

Makiya, Kanan. *Cruelty and Silence: War, Tyranny, Uprising, and the Arab World.* New York: Norton, 1994.

———. *Republic of Fear.* Los Angeles: University of California Press, 1998.

Mann, Thomas. *Achtung, Europa! 1933–1938.* Frankfurt am Main: S. Fischer, 1995.

Minc, Alain. "Terrorism of the Spirit." Trans. Kathy Ackerman. *Telos* 121 (Fall 2001): 143–45.

Moran, Daniel. "Restraints on Violence and the Reconstruction of International Order after 1945." In *War and Terror,* ed. Frank Trommler and Michael Geyer. Washington: American Institute for Contemporary German Studies. Forthcoming.

Natteau, Nicholas. *Saddam over Iraq: How Much Longer? A Study of the Ba'thist Destruction of Iraqi Civil Society and the Prospects for Its Rebirth.* Masters Thesis, Boston University, 1997. www.joric.com/Saddam/Saddam.htm.

Nullis, Claire. "Report: Arab Economies Need Reform." *Washington Times,* September 8, 2002.

Pew Global Attitudes Project. *Views of a Changing World, June 2003.* Washington, D.C.: Pew Research Center for the People and the Press, 2003.

Revel, Jean-François. *L'obsession anti-américaine: Son fonctionnement, ses causes, ses inconséquences.* Paris: Plon, 2002.

Roger, Philippe. *L'ennemi américain: Généalogie de l'antiamericanisme française.* Paris: Seuil, 2002.

Roy, Arundhati. *The Cost of Living.* New York: Modern Library, 1999.

————. *The God of Small Things.* New York: Harper, 1998.

————. *Power Politics.* Cambridge: South End Press, 2001.

Rushdie, Salman. "February 2002: Anti-Americanism." In Rushdie, *Step across This Line: Collected Nonfiction 1992–2002.* New York: Random House, 2002.

Safire, William. "The German Problem," *New York Times*, September 19, 2002. A35.

Shlapentokh, Vladmir, and Joshua Woods. *America's Image Abroad.* Forthcoming.

Smith, Tom W., and Lars Jarkko. "National Pride in Cross-National Perspective." Paper of the National Opinion Research Center. University of Chicago, April 2001. http://www.issp.org/paper.htm.

Zadek, Peter. "Kulturkampf? Ich bin dabei." Interview in *Der Spiegel*, July 14, 2003.

Zantop, Susan. *Colonial Fantasies: Conquest, Family, and Nation in Precolonial Germany, 1770–1870.* Durham: Duke University Press, 1997.

Zelikow, Philip, and Condoleezza Rice. *Germany Unified and Europe Transformed: A Study in Statecraft.* Cambridge: Harvard University Press, 1995.

Index ❖

ass. living for. w/
Turkish numu